GAME DAY
TENNESSEE FOOTBALL

GAME DAY
TENNESSEE FOOTBALL

*The Greatest Games, Players, Coaches and Teams
in the Glorious Tradition of Volunteer Football*

TRIUMPH
BOOKS
CHICAGO

Athlon Sports
AMERICA'S PREMIER SPORTS ANNUALS

Library of Congress Control Number: 2006924580

This book is available in quantity at special discounts for your group or organization. For further information, contact:

Triumph Books
542 South Dearborn Street
Suite 750
Chicago, Illinois 60605
(312) 939-3330
Fax (312) 663-3557

CONTRIBUTING WRITERS: Mike Griffith, Nathan Kirkham

EDITOR: Rob Doster

PHOTO EDITOR: Tim Clark
PHOTO ASSISTANT: Danny Murphy

DESIGN: Anderson Thomas Design
PRODUCTION: Odds & Ends Multimedia

PHOTO CREDITS: Athlon Sports Archive, Tennessee Sports Information, AP/Wide World Photos

Printed in U.S.A.

ISBN-13: 978-1-57243-878-1
ISBN-10: 1-57243-878-9

CONTENTS

Foreword

In 1997, when it came time to declare whether I would stay at the University of Tennessee for my senior season, there was plenty of conjecture in the media about which direction I would take.

For this reason or that, it was reported, I would jump to the NFL. For this reason or that, it was countered, I would remain in school for one more year. When all was said and done, the bottom line was that I had enjoyed my previous three seasons so much, I wanted one more chance to drink in the full experience of being a Tennessee Vol.

That reason alone overcame any thoughts to the contrary. And when you get right down to it, the matchless Tennessee fans were the decisive factor in my choosing to stick around Knoxville for the 1997 season.

I say "matchless fans" while understanding that Georgia and Alabama and Auburn, among others, would make equal claim about the level of their support. But that's a debate I would happily take on. There is nothing quite like being at a Tennessee home game on a crisp autumn Saturday afternoon.

No matter who our opponent was, regardless of the weather, hours before the game, Tennessee fans began the trek to Neyland Stadium. By kickoff time, 107,000 fans invariably were in their seats, primed and ready to

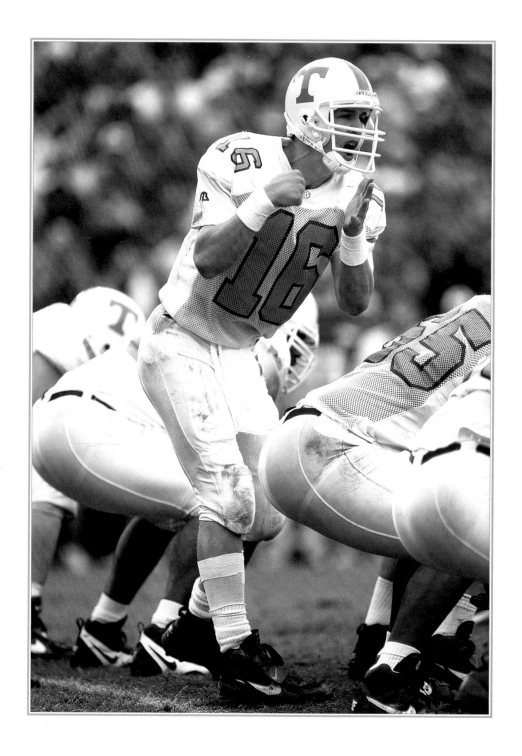

cheer us to victory. Now, wherever I go, talking to other NFL players, I tell them that one time before they depart this earth, they owe it to themselves to attend a game at Neyland Stadium.

They need to experience the full flavor of the day: watch fans disembark at the dock harboring the Vol Navy, tailgate or stop by Calhoun's on the river before the game, resume tailgating as the sun sets over Knoxville and perhaps a visit to Ye Olde Steakhouse or one of the city's other good restaurants later in the evening.

Much of the support from Tennessee fans stems from their knowledge of the university's football history, which is something that I picked up during my four years on campus. When I enrolled at UT in 1994, my familiarity with Vol football's past was bare-bones. I was aware of the significant roles people like General Neyland, Reggie White and Doug Atkins played in establishing the school as a national powerhouse, but not a whole lot more.

As a person who has always reveled in the tradition and lore of college football, I took a keen interest during my four years in Knoxville in expanding my knowledge of Big Orange football. I read about the great players and coaches, the championship years and the rivalries that began more than a century ago and which endure today. What an incredible story it is!

As much as anything else, though, my fondest and most lasting memory of UT was the unbelievable level of devotion its fans express for the program. During the 2005 season the university honored me by retiring my uniform number in a ceremony before the South Carolina game.

Standing at midfield, my wife and parents at my side, I was overwhelmed by the welcome accorded to me on my return to campus by the crowd packed into Neyland Stadium that afternoon. Overwhelmed, yes, but not surprised by the support.

For myself, and for all those hundreds of thousands of other Tennessee fans, the book you are reading offers a nostalgic journey through the decades in the proud history of a college football program that is second to none in achievement and in fan loyalty.

—Peyton Manning

Introduction

The images are unforgettable and too numerous to count.

The orange-clad Volunteers bursting through the *T* as more than 100,000 citizens of Vol Nation roar themselves hoarse. Phillip Fulmer and the 1998 Vols hoisting the championship hardware. Peyton Manning leading the Pride of the Southland Band in the playing of "Rocky Top" after his final regular-season game. Condredge Holloway slithering his way through impossibly small openings in the defense on his way to pay dirt. John Ward marking off the yardage on another touchdown run before exclaiming, "Give...him...six!" Dewey Warren to Richmond Flowers. Hank Lauricella, Doug Atkins, Gene McEver. General Neyland.

In this book, we've attempted to distill the pageantry and drama of Tennessee football into the pages that follow. It's a daunting task. No program in the country inspires the loyalty and passion that Tennessee football exacts from its fans. And with good reason.

Through the words and images we present here, you can get a taste of what Tennessee football is all about. If you're a true Tennessee fan, we can guarantee a few goose bumps by the time you're finished.

So let's get started. As has been said many times over: "It's football time in Tennessee!"

TRADITIONS AND PAGEANTRY

The traditions and pageantry of Tennessee football are rich and deep. They are passed down from generation to generation: a sense of duty, Southern pride, and, of course, an undying love for Tennessee football.

The Colors

Orange and white. The unusual pairing tells you plenty about a streak of independence common to Tennesseans. Most schools using orange as a school color go with a darker shade not occurring in nature. The majority of those will pair their "orange" with a darker color because graphic designers will tell you orange and white don't offer enough contrast. Television commentators hate white numerals on orange jerseys because it makes for a long day for even the most eagle-eyed spotter. Tennessee fans will offer up some choice words for all the naysayers—and then rush to the store to brighten up their closet with some more orange and white garb.

It's a good thing the Volunteers are known for a physical, rough-and-tumble style of football because their school colors pay homage to a flower. That's right—the orange and white pairing was selected by Charles Moore, a member of Tennessee's first football team in 1891, because it reminded him of the common American daisy that graced the Hill in his day, just a Hail Mary from the north end zone. The football team first donned the famous orange jersey against Emory and Henry in 1922, a game the Vols won 50–0.

The Nickname

What's a Volunteer? It's not your run-of-the-mill school nickname. The proud legacy of the Volunteer calls Tennessee student-athletes to compete at an elevated standard when the stakes are highest. A Volunteer is the bravest breed of human from the boldest nation on Earth, fiercely proud to call Tennessee home, whether the battle lies within its borders or in a land far away. The Volunteers rose to defeat the British early in our nation's history, from the Overmountain Men in the Revolutionary War to Andrew "Old Hickory" Jackson's skillful defense of New Orleans in the War of 1812. No matter how fearsome the foe, whether outnumbered like David Crockett and his courageous Volunteers at the Alamo or Sergeant Alvin York's individual heroics against the Germans in World War I, a Volunteer is always ready when his homeland calls. Every time since the nation's birth to this very day, when the U.S. needs an extraordinary effort to brush back the dark curtain of hopelessness, the Tennessee Volunteers have been available. The bravery, heroism, wisdom and ferocity of the Volunteers place them on a pedestal of great American legends.

The Helmet

Like its peers at the top of the college football world, Tennessee's familiar football helmet is iconic. Not unlike Notre Dame's golden glow or Michigan's eye-catching design, the *T* emblazoned on the side of the Vols' headgear leaves no doubt as to affiliation. Love them or hate them, it doesn't take long to recognize when the Volunteers are on TV again.

With the orange power *T* logo affixed to both sides of a white helmet with an orange stripe down the center, the basic design hasn't changed much since 1964, when head coach Doug Dickey arrived in Knoxville. Before 1964, the design featured white helmets with an orange stripe down the middle, with just two exceptions: in 1962, orange numerals were added to the sides of the helmets, and in 1963, the design remained the same except black numerals were used.

Marching Band

The Pride of the Southland Marching Band adds to Tennessee's considerable reputation as a state richly marinated in musical history. Dr. Gary Sousa, director of bands, heads a program employing the services of more than 400 musicians in all bands. The Pride of the Southland Marching Band marks the best-known unit in the program. The band is known for its precision pregame and half-time formations stepping off 100 yards of turf in Neyland Stadium—and for its numerous renditions of "Rocky Top."

First organized after the conclusion of the Civil War, the band offered war-weary Knoxvillians a welcome change from musket balls to music. In time, the Pride of the Southland Band became one of the state's most respected musical ambassadors, and it has represented the state of Tennessee for the last 40 years at 10 consecutive presidential inaugurations. From Dwight D. Eisenhower to George W. Bush, the Pride of the Southland Band has provided pomp and pageantry befitting such a ceremony.

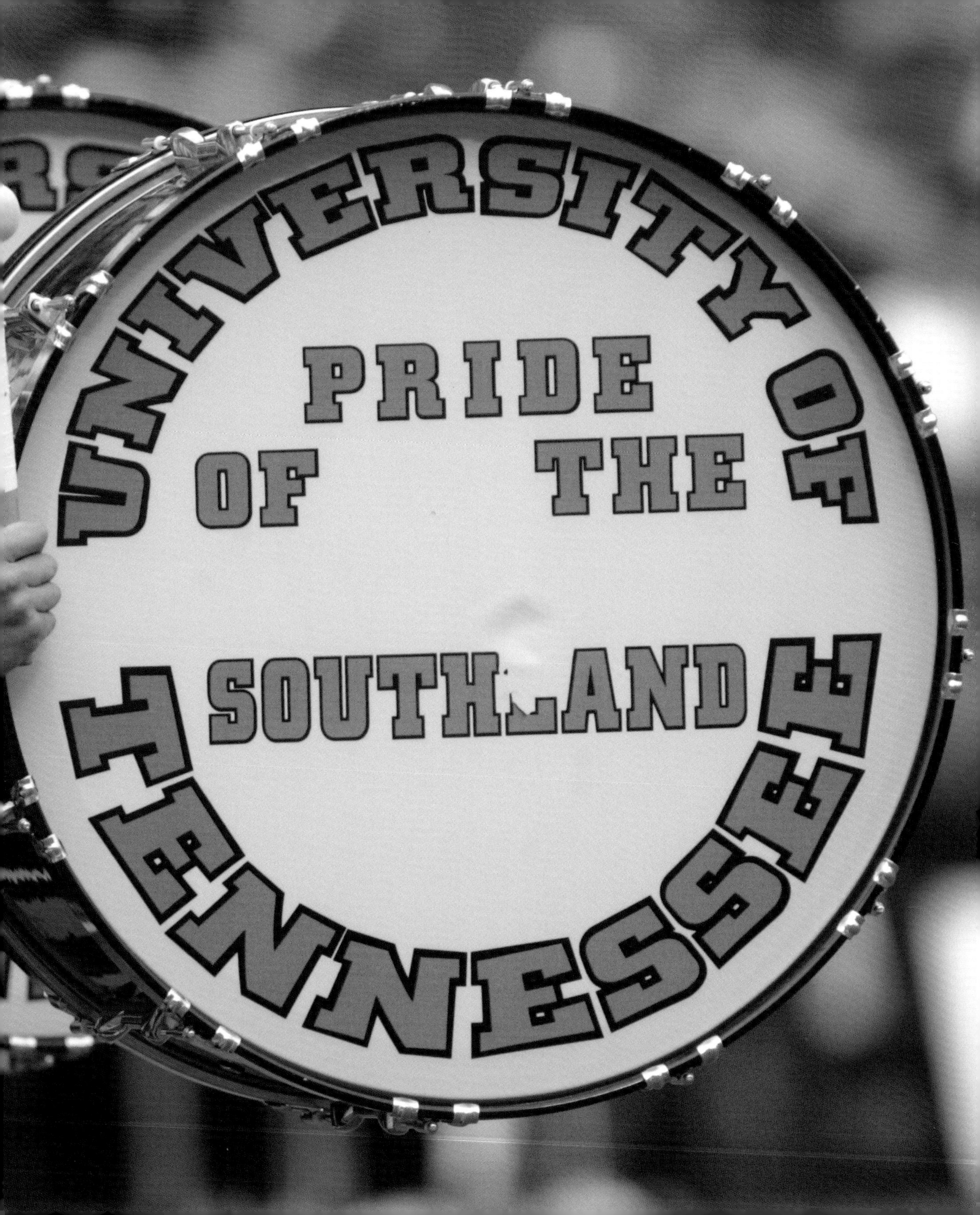
UNIVERSITY OF
PRIDE
OF THE
SOUTHLAND
TENNESSEE

VolWalk

Tennessee spirit and pageantry is on display each Saturday two and a half hours before kickoff when the Volunteers make their march amid thousands of orange-and-white clad fans who line the trail. The Tennessee players walk in loose ranks from the Neyland-Thompson Sports Center, down Volunteer Boulevard, through Peyton Manning Pass and finally into Neyland Stadium where the weekend's enemy awaits them.

The band leads the way, blasting "Rocky Top" and stepping high, whetting the appetite of the early arriving fans who can't bear to prolong the anticipation of another Volunteer victory.

The heroes follow the band, most dressed in suits or ties, carrying their uniforms in a duffel bag as they head for battle.

In addition to the goodwill, the VolWalk produces by allowing fans an up-close look at the players without helmets and shoulder pads, and the tradition has also played a role in Tennessee's successful recruiting.

Most of the potential signees in for official visits take part in the VolWalk, allowing them to have an opportunity to see and feel how great it can be to be a Tennessee Volunteer.

—— Vol Navy ——

George Mooney, a former Tennessee broadcaster, first navigated his small run-about vessel down the Tennessee River before a 1962 Volunteers football game. It was an idea whose time had come. It quickly caught on, and thus was born the Volunteer Navy, a floating tailgate party that crowds the Tennessee River in the shadow of Neyland Stadium. Thousands of Tennessee football fans arrive at Neyland Stadium via the river, docking their boats along Neyland Drive before hiking the final two blocks on foot.

Rocky Top

Wish that I was on ol' Rocky Top
Down in the Tennessee hills;
Ain't no smoggy smoke on Rocky Top,
Ain't no telephone bills.
Once I had a girl on Rocky Top,
Half bear, other half cat;
Wild as a mink, but sweet as soda pop,
I still dream about that.

(chorus)
Rocky Top, you'll always be
Home sweet home to me;
Good ol' Rocky Top—
Rocky Top Tennessee, Rocky Top Tennessee.

Once two strangers climbed ol' Rocky Top,
Lookin' for a moonshine still;
Strangers ain't come down from Rocky Top,
Reckon they never will.
Corn won't grow at all on Rocky Top,
Dirt's too rocky by far;
That's why all the folks on Rocky Top
Get their corn from a jar.
(chorus)
I've had years of cramped-up city life,
Trapped like a duck in a pen;
All I know is it's a pity life
Can't be simple again.
(chorus)

"Rocky Top"

The foot-stompin' jingle rouses Tennessee fans each time it's played, be it at Neyland Stadium, Thompson-Boling Arena, Lindsey Nelson Stadium or perhaps even your local pub. Felice and Boudleaux Bryant wrote the song in 10 minutes at the Gatlinburg Inn in 1967. The song features just five basic chords, and the title is repeated 19 times in the song. It was first played as part of a country music show at the 1972 Tennessee-Alabama game.

Neyland Stadium

The home of the Volunteers' football Saturdays ranks number three in the nation by its capacity, but few Tennessee fans would place it anywhere but number one in their hearts.

The 104,079-seat stadium named after Tennessee's fabled coach, General Robert R. Neyland, has undergone 16 expansions since its original conception as Shields-Watkins Field in 1921. The Volunteers turned to artificial turf in 1968 before returning to natural grass in 1994.

The first south end upper deck expansion, completed in 1972, brought with it nighttime football when the Volunteers opened the season with a game against Penn State.

Neyland Stadium is currently being renovated again as the Volunteers' administration continues its quest to keep the facility at the top of the heap.

Checkerboard End Zones

The orange and white checkerboard end zones first appeared in 1964, the first year of current athletic director Doug Dickey's coaching tenure. They disappeared in 1968, with the introduction of an artificial playing surface, then reappeared in 1989, where they remain to this day.

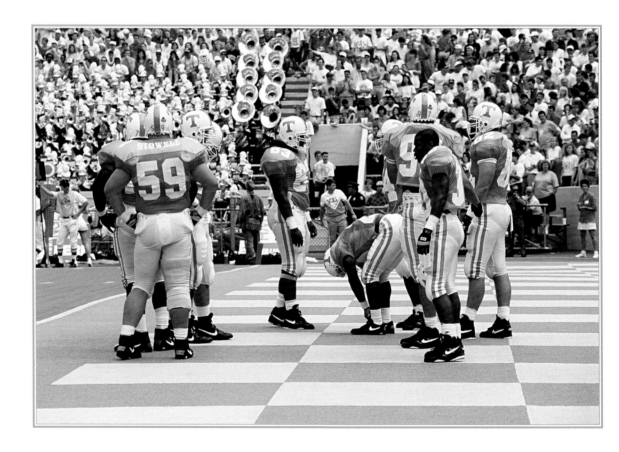

Smokey the Bluetick Coonhound

Serving as mascot for the Volunteer football team since 1953 is Smokey the bluetick coonhound. The late Reverend Bill Brooks' prizewinner served as Smokey I in 1953 and 1954. Smokey VIII was the winningest Smokey, sporting a record of 91–22 (.805), with two SEC titles and the 1998 national championship. The Tennessee-bred canine currently leading the Vols through the *T* prior to each home game and stalking the sidelines is Smokey IX.

Fight Song

No, the official fight song is not the infectious "Rocky Top." That honor belongs to "Here's to Old Tennessee (Down the Field)." The official fight song captures much about the character of campus and the state's military heritage. The marriage of Gwen Sweet's words and Chas. Fielder's arrangement was copyrighted in 1939, a year that saw the Vols take the SEC title and hold all 10 regular-season opponents scoreless. A model of efficiency, "Down the Field" pays tribute to Tennessee football, fighting, orange and white, marching, the Spirit of the Hill, courage and loyalty in a mere 78 words. The Pride of the Southland Band gives the song an honored place in its pregame show before every home game.

Here's to Old Tennessee (Down the Field)

Here's to old Tennessee

Ne'er shall we sever

We pledge our loyalty

For ever and ever

Backing her football team

Faltering never

Cheer and fight with all your might

For Tennessee!

Running through the *T*

In the culmination of a pregame spectacle unrivaled in college athletics, Tennessee's football team piles into a crowded tunnel as the Pride of the Southland Band wraps up its pregame show. The players are unable to see their rivals or the hysteria building to a fever pitch around them. But they can hear it building louder and louder. And they can feel it, as the venerable House that Neyland Built shakes and rumbles its steel skeleton as the fanatics await the entry of their heroes. With 107,000 fans whipped into a frenzy, The Pride of the Southland Band forms the giant *T* that serves as a runway as the players sprint onto the field bathed in the admiration of the Volunteer nation. With mascot Smokey up front sniffing out a true trail, head coach Phillip Fulmer leads his charges up the base of the *T* and hangs a

left to take up residence on the Tennessee sideline.

The *T* was one of head coach Doug Dickey's innovations. In 1965, Dickey moved the Tennessee bench from the east sideline, its current location, to the west sideline. The move allowed the Vols to make the ceremonious entry from their dressing room, which then exited at the 50-yard line on the east side, through the *T* formed east to west, and onto the west sideline. In 1983, a new dressing room was built underneath the north end zone stands. In response, the *T*, thankfully a flexible letter, was moved to its current location, running north to south, though players took a right to the west sideline. When the home bench returned to the east sideline, the only change necessary was a left turn instead of a right.

——— John Ward ———

More than a play-by-play announcer, John Ward earned his position as a Tennessee institution by painting a vivid picture of Appalachia's grandest autumn drama for 31 seasons. From 1968 to 1998, Ward and color analyst Bill Anderson dutifully took their positions in the press box and brought fall's action into living rooms across the Volunteer State. Ward's delightful descriptions proved accurate, colorful and endearing.

Ward began his football announcing career in a world offering precious little college football television coverage. It's quite a rarity today not to be able to watch the football Vols on television, but that wasn't always the case. For those unfortunates unable to attend the game, Ward served as the eyes and ears of Volunteer fans far and wide. He was so esteemed that even when television games became commonplace, families across the state preferred to turn down the television sound and turned up Ward and Anderson to tell the story of the day with substance and style. His oft-imitated signature phrases—"Give Him Six!" and "It's Football Time in Tennessee!"—testified that Ward's hero status was alive and well in countless ragtag backyard games from Mountain City to Memphis. To millions of Tennessee fans, Ward was Tennessee football, even more than some of the legendary coaches who cast a long shadow stalking Tennessee's sideline in his tenure. His last football game befitted his charmed run. On January 4, 1999, as the sun sank low in the Arizona desert, televisions across the Volunteer State were silenced and radios crackled to life as Ward masterfully detailed Tennessee's Fiesta Bowl win over Florida State and its return to college football's promised land.

Alma Mater

Verse I

On a hallowed hill in Tennessee

Like a beacon shining bright

The stately walls of old U.T.

Rise glorious to the sight.

Refrain

So here's to you, old Tennessee

Our alma mater true.

We pledge in love and harmony

Our loyalty to you.

Verse II

What torches kindled at that flame

Have passed from hand to hand.

What hearts cemented in that name

Bind land to stranger land.

Refrain

So here's to you, old Tennessee

Our alma mater true.

We pledge in love and harmony

Our loyalty to you.

Verse III

O, ever as we strive to rise

On life's unresting stream

Dear Alma Mater, may our eyes

Be lifted to that gleam.

Refrain

So here's to you, old Tennessee

Our alma mater true.

We pledge in love and harmony

Our loyalty to you.

THE GREATEST PLAYERS

Tennessee's roster of greats reads like a who's who of college football legends. The names are familiar to fans of college football, and for the fans of the Vols' rivals, they still bring a shiver of dread. Here are some of the stars who have shone brightest during their tenures in Knoxville.

Tennessee has had so many national award winners, so many great players, that they can't all be included here, which is why the following list should be considered representative, not definitive. We start with the Hall of Famers.

——— Tennesee Players ———
in the College Football Hall of Fame

NATHAN DOUGHERTY
Guard, 1906–1909
Inducted 1967

A 6'2", 185-pound guard, Dougherty was nicknamed "the Big One." He played fullback part time and scored a touchdown in UT's 15–0 win over Georgia in 1907. He also returned a kickoff for a touchdown in 1908. He was two-year All-Southern and team captain in 1909. Later, as chairman of Tennessee's Athletic Council, Dougherty was responsible for bringing Bob Neyland to Knoxville as head coach.

GENE MCEVER
Halfback, 1928–1929, 1931
Inducted 1954

McEver was the personification of power football in his day. Stocky, strong and fast, he was nicknamed "the Wild Bull." McEver was a unanimous All-America halfback for three years: 1928, 1929 and 1931. (Knee surgery kept him sidelined for 1930.) In 1929, he led all of college football in scoring with 130 points. His 98-yard kickoff return against Alabama in 1928 helped thrust the Vols into the nation's consciousness.

BEATTIE FEATHERS
Halfback, 1931–1933
Inducted 1955

A halfback on Neyland's great teams of the early 1930s, William Beattie Feathers seemed to fly through opposing defenses. He was a threat to score from anywhere on the field. In Tennessee's 7–3 win over Alabama in 1932, he averaged 48 yards on 21 punts and ran for the game's only touchdown. He was the SEC MVP and All-America in 1933. As a halfback with the Chicago Bears in 1934, Feathers set an NFL single-season record with 8.4 yards per carry, a mark that still stands.

BOBBY DODD
Quarterback, 1928–1930
Inducted 1959 (player), 1993 (coach)

As the quarterback of Tennessee's famous Hack, Mack and Dodd backfield of 1928–1930, Bobby Dodd guided the Vols to a 27–1–2 record and made All-America in 1930. Like his coach, Bob Neyland, Dodd has a stadium named after him—at Georgia Tech, where he was head coach for 22 years (1945–1966) and won 71 percent of his games. Dodd is one of only three men enshrined in the College Football Hall of Fame as both a player and a coach.

HERMAN HICKMAN
Guard, 1929–1931
Inducted 1959

Up through his playing days at Tennessee (1929–1931), Herman Hickman ranked with Yale's Pudge Heffelfinger as the greatest guards ever to play the game. Hickman's legendary speed, power and agility made him the most famous lineman in Southern football. He could outrun almost all of his teammates. He was human road grader on offense, and on defense, he left opposing blockers and ball carriers together in heaps on the ground. After playing professionally for three years, Hickman later went on to coach at both Army and Yale.

BOB SUFFRIDGE
Guard, 1938–1940
Inducted 1961

Bob Suffridge is the only three-time consensus All-American in Tennessee history. With Suffridge at guard, the Vols plowed through three straight regular-season slates without a loss. Not particularly big for a guard (6'1", 185 pounds) even in his day, Suffridge boasted a charge that has been compared to the thrust of a jet engine. According to Neyland: "Suff had the quickest and most powerful defensive charge of any lineman I've ever seen. He never made a bad play." He was arguably the best ever of the pulling single-wing guards.

GEORGE CAFEGO
Tailback, 1937–1939
Inducted 1969

George "Bad News" Cafego was a two-year All-America single-wing tailback for some of Neyland's greatest teams. Of Cafego, the immortal coach remarked: "In practice he couldn't do anything right. But for two hours on Saturday afternoons he did everything an All-American is supposed to do." Cafego's powerful, churning legs made him hard to bring down. He also possessed blinding speed and was a deadly accurate passer. Cafego was the SEC Player of the Year in 1938, when the Volunteers went 11–0. Later in life, Cafego spent 30 years as an assistant football coach at his alma mater.

BOWDEN WYATT

End, 1936–1938

Inducted 1972 (player), 1997 (coach)

As a senior in 1938, Bowden Wyatt was captain of the 11–0 Tennessee squad. He was an All-SEC and All-America end that year, in addition to his duties as placekicker. He went on to an illustrious head coaching career at Wyoming, Arkansas and Tennessee. Along with Amos Alonzo Stagg and fellow Vol Bobby Dodd, Wyatt ranks as one of just three men in the College Football Hall of Fame as both a player and a coach.

ED MOLINSKI
Guard, 1938–1940
Inducted 1990

Molinski teamed with Bob Suffridge to form possibly the top guard combo of all time through the halcyon days of 1938, 1939 and 1940. He was a key to the Tennessee defense that made shutouts a regular occurrence, including the unscored-upon unit of 1939. Molinski was All-SEC and All-America in 1939 and 1940.

HANK LAURICELLA
Tailback, 1949–1951
Inducted 1981

Lauricella, a New Orleans native, was an All-SEC selection in 1950 and an All-American in 1951, when he finished as runner-up in the Heisman voting behind Princeton's Dick Kazmaier. Lauricella was the ultimate single-wing tailback—a position made famous at UT during Neyland's tenure. Lauricella's shining moment as a Vol came in the 1951 Cotton Bowl game when he weaved through the Texas defense for 75 yards to set up the first touchdown of the day in the Vols' 20–14 victory. He then proceeded to lead Tennessee to its first consensus national title the following season.

JOHN MICHELS
Guard, 1950–1952
Inducted 1996

John Michels may be overshadowed by the likes of Suffridge, Molinski, Dougherty and Hickman as UT guards, but as a blocker he took a back seat to none. He was All-SEC in 1951 and All-America in 1952. Tennessee won 27 of 32 games with Michels in the lineup. He later went on to a career as an assistant coach in the NFL. He was on the staff of the Minnesota Vikings for 27 years, including four Super Bowl campaigns.

DOUG ATKINS
End, 1950–1952
Inducted 1985

If Doug Atkins isn't the scariest defensive end ever to play organized football, he is certainly in the top three. He was All-SEC in 1951, All-America in 1952 and the first-round draft pick of the Chicago Bears in 1953. Atkins was voted the SEC Player of the Quarter Century (1950–1974) by the Football Writers Association. He is the only UT Vol in both the College and Pro Football Halls of Fame.

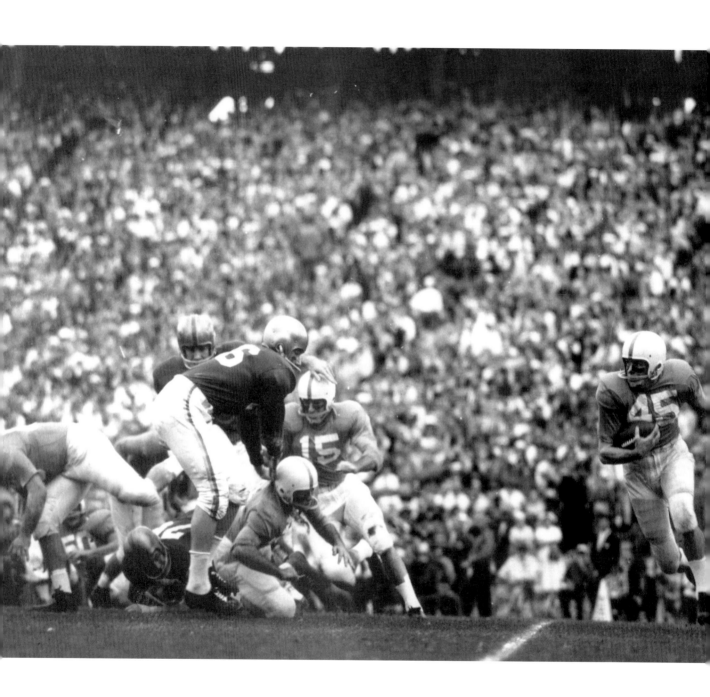

Majors (45), with teammates Buddy Cruze and John Gordy.

JOHNNY MAJORS
Tailback, 1954–1956
Inducted 1987

Johnny Majors finished second in the Heisman voting after leading Tennessee to a 10–1 record in 1956. (Paul Hornung of 2–8 Notre Dame won it.) Through his career, Majors led the Vols in passing, rushing, scoring, punting, punt returns and kickoff returns. He was a two-time SEC Player of the Year, in 1955 and 1956. After his playing career, Majors held head coaching offices at Iowa State, Pittsburgh and UT, winning a national title in 1976 at Pitt.

BOB JOHNSON
Center, 1965–1967
Inducted 1989

Bob Johnson was a two-time All-America center for Tennessee in 1966 and 1967, captaining coach Doug Dickey's 1967 squad that won a share of the national championship. A member of the SEC All-Quarter Century team, Johnson also was an Academic All-American and recipient of the National Football Foundation Post-Graduate Scholarship in 1967. He was the first overall NFL Draft choice in 1968, taken by the expansion Cincinnati Bengals.

FRANK EMANUEL
Linebacker, 1963–1965
Inducted 2004

Emanuel played a key role in helping to revive the Tennessee football program in the early 1960s. A consensus First Team All-American, Emanuel led the Vols to an 8–1–2 record and a Bluebonnet Bowl victory in 1965—their first bowl appearance in eight years. Emanuel was the first draft choice of the Miami Dolphins and was featured on the cover of *Sports Illustrated* as an example of the bidding war for players between the NFL and the AFL.

STEVE DELONG

Middle Guard, 1962–1964

Inducted 1993

Steve DeLong was a two-time All-American in 1963 and 1964, and team captain in 1964. Tennessee's football fortunes were on a down cycle in DeLong's senior year, but that didn't deter the Norfolk, Virginia, native from dominating games at his middle guard position. He took home the Outland Trophy as the nation's best interior lineman and was a first-round draft pick in 1965.

STEVE KINER
Linebacker, 1967–1969
Inducted 1999

Bear Bryant once compared Steve Kiner to former 'Bama great Lee Roy Jordan. Kiner was one of the finest linebackers the SEC ever produced. The conference's Sophomore of the Year in 1967, Kiner was an All-American in 1968 and 1969. He possessed more speed than most running backs and was the toughest linebacker in the game during his day.

REGGIE WHITE
Defensive Tackle, 1980–1983
Inducted 2002

It might require a knowledge of history to recognize the names of some of Tennessee's Hall of Famers, but anybody who is old enough to drive a car and vote knows Reggie White, the Vols' latest inductee. The Minister of Defense holds school records for sacks in a single season with 15 in 1983 and in a career with 32. He holds the NFL record for career sacks with 192.5. In 1983, White was the SEC Player of the Year and an All-American.

—————— Other Tennessee Greats ——————

CONDREDGE HOLLOWAY
Quarterback, 1972–1974

Condredge Holloway threw for well over 3,000 yards as a quarterback at Tennessee, and he may be even better remembered as a dazzling open-field runner. But his greatest legacy is the one he left as the first black quarterback in the history of the Southeastern Conference. Holloway also was a gifted baseball player, and turned down a lucrative offer from the Montreal Expos to remain at UT. After graduation, Holloway enjoyed a long and successful career in the Canadian Football League.

The "Huntsville Houdini" was one of the most exciting players in SEC history.

PEYTON MANNING
Quarterback, 1994–1997

Peyton Manning's return home from the Downtown Athletic Club without the 1997 Heisman Trophy was hard to figure. He had just led the Vols to an 11–2 record and the SEC title. He finished his career having rewritten the school passing record book and extensively edited the SEC records. He left Knoxville in possession of conference marks for career wins as a starter, completions, completion percentage, passing yards and total offense, among others. He held NCAA records for lowest interception percentage for a season and career, and he ranked third in NCAA history in passing yards and total offense. He won the 1997 Davey O'Brien and Johnny Unitas Awards, was the SEC Player of the Year and was a unanimous All-American.

PEERLESS PRICE
Wide Receiver, 1995–1998

Price was the ultimate deep threat for the Vols during the 1998 title run, and he always came through in the clutch. Against Alabama, Price had a 100-yard kickoff return to break open the game. In the SEC Championship Game win over Mississippi State, Price reeled in an over-the-shoulder 41-yard TD pass, and he was the MVP of the 23–16 win over Florida State in the 1998 title game with four receptions for 199 yards and a touchdown.

AL WILSON
Linebacker, 1995–1998

Wilson is the standard by which all modern-era UT linebackers are measured. Tough, mean and aggressive between the lines, Wilson was the unquestioned leader of the 1998 national championship team. In the 20–17 overtime win over Florida, Wilson had 13 tackles and three forced fumbles, and he played most of the rest of the season with a shoulder that would regularly pop out of place.

"If Al Wilson slapped your mama, you'd ask her what she did to deserve it." —TEAMMATE NEIL JOHNSON, ON THE RESPECT WILSON COMMANDED FROM HIS TEAMMATES

TEE MARTIN
Quarterback, 1996–1999

Martin entrenched himself in UT history by leading the Vols to a perfect 13–0 record and the 1998 national championship. He finished his career 13–0 as a starter in games played at Neyland Stadium. Martin's big arm and mobility were key on two of Tennessee's signature plays during his tenure: the bootleg and deep passes to receivers Peerless Price and Cedrick Wilson. Like Peyton Manning, Martin has a wax figurine of his likeness in the Vols' Hall of Fame room and a street named after him near the stadium.

DEON GRANT
Free Safety, 1996–1999

Grant will be remembered as one of the greatest athletes to grace the UT secondary, playing "center field" at free safety, to enable the Vols to play what amounted to an eight-man front. Grant's TD-saving fourth quarter interception against Florida, when he said, "The angels lifted me," will forever be remembered as a keystone play to the 1998 national championship season. Grant went on to win the SEC's Defensive Player of the Year award in 1999 with nine interceptions.

JAMAL LEWIS
Running Back, 1997–1999

"Give the Ball to Jamal" was a familiar refrain among Vols' fans during this powerful running back's tenure. Lewis' rare blend of power and speed enabled him to rush for a UT freshman-record 1,364 yards during the 1997 season and lead the Vols to the SEC Championship and an Orange Bowl appearance. Lewis was key early in the 1998 national title run before he suffered a season-ending knee injury the fourth game of the season against Auburn.

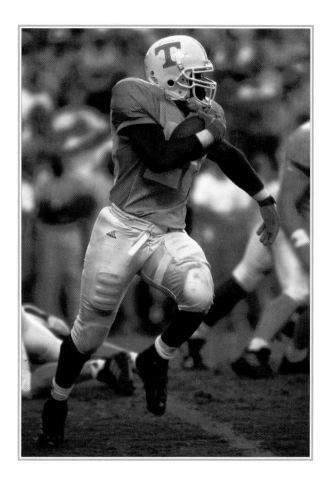

TRAVIS HENRY
Tailback, 1997–2000

Known to Tennessee fans as "the Cheese," Henry quickly became a fan favorite with his powerful bursts into scrimmage and pile-moving ways. It was Henry who put the Vols on his shoulders in the final minutes of Tennessee's miraculous 28–24 come-from behind win over Arkansas, powering his way through the Hogs and into the end zone.

Henry finished his career as the school's all-time leading rusher with 3,078 yards on 556 carries and a career 5.5 yards-per-carry rushing average.

JOHN HENDERSON
Defensive Tackle, 1999–2001

John Henderson brought the 2000 Outland Trophy home to Tennessee and was a finalist for the 2001 hardware despite fighting through injuries like a trooper. In 2000, his second year as a starter, the Nashville native recorded 71 tackles and 12 sacks, forced four fumbles and recovered three. He added another 39 stops and 4.5 sacks during his injury-shortened 2001 campaign. Big John was a two-year All-American, plugging the middle for the vaunted Vol defense.

CASEY CLAUSEN
Quarterback, 2000–2003

The school's second all-time leading passer, Clausen slew the mighty Florida Gators at the Swamp in consecutive road trips, giving UT its first wins in Gainesville since Phillip Fulmer was a player in 1971. What Clausen—a.k.a. "the Iceman"—lacked in athleticism, he made up for with poise, toughness and competitive fire. In his first start as a true freshman, Clausen beat Alabama on the road with a near-flawless 17-of-24, two-TD passing performance that included one play where he continued to fight for yardage in a pileup despite his helmet having been torn off.

THE COACHES

It has taken the leadership of great men to produce the legacy and tradition that embody Tennessee football. Two Vol coaches in particular stand among the greats the game has produced.

General Robert R. Neyland

General Robert R. Neyland transformed the Volunteer program from a football backwater to a colossus on the banks of the Tennessee River. Neyland (pronounced KNEE-land) was Paul Bunyan with a whistle, a legend larger than life. All too often the essence of a legend gets choked out, overtaken by the kudzu of embellishment, as the truth drifts away through the mists of memory. Neyland's 21 years (1926–1934, 1936–1940 and 1946–1952) at the Vol helm need no embellishment.

A lifelong friend of General Douglas MacArthur, Brigadier General Neyland ran his football team with military precision. "The

same cardinal rules apply to both," Neyland said. The general could never separate his great passions of athletics and the military. The two breaks in his Tennessee coaching career were at the insistence of the Army, when he was sent to Panama's canal zone in 1935 and to the China-Burma-India theater in World War II.

After a sterling athletic and academic experience at West Point, he arrived on the Hill in 1925 as an Army captain, ROTC instructor and backfield coach with a starting salary of $600 a year. He would leave as Tennessee's most famous football coach. Neyland compiled an impressive record of 173–31–12 during 21 seasons as the Vols' general. Neyland piloted

Tennessee to four national championships (1938, 1940, 1950 and 1951-consensus) and seven conference crowns. Neyland's 1939 squad was the last in the nation to hold all regular-season opponents scoreless. His team still holds the NCAA record for holding opponents scoreless for 71 consecutive quarters.

Neyland fashioned stingy, hard-nosed defenses and demanded precision in all facets of the kicking game. His teams shut out 112 of 216 opponents. He felt no such fondness for offense but was known for an efficient single-wing attack. He prized field position, a belief firmly rooted in West Point doctrine. Herman Hickman, who played guard skillfully for the General and became a fine coach in his own

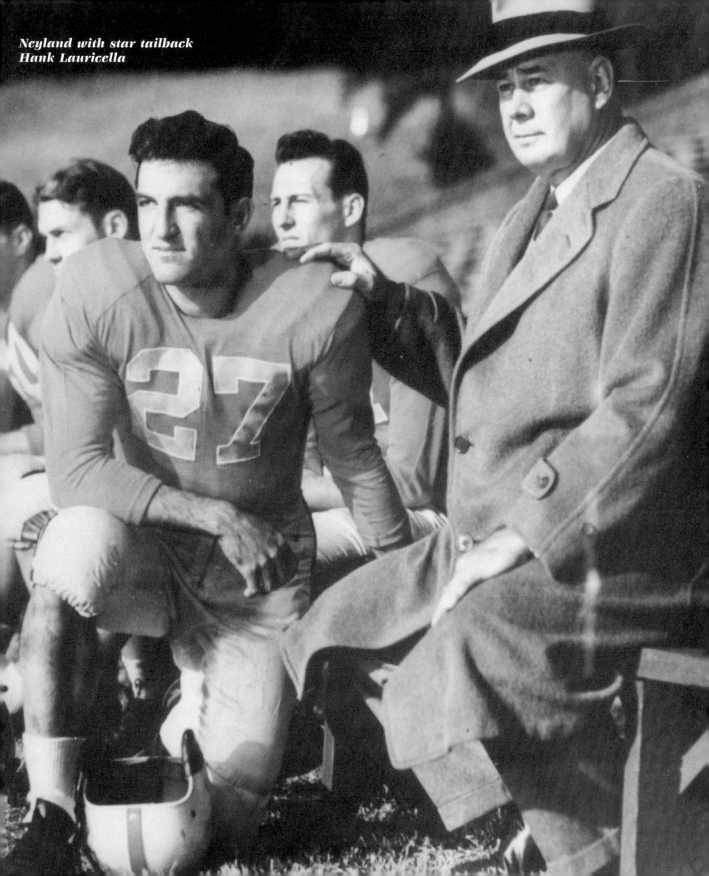

*Neyland with star tailback
Hank Lauricella*

NEYLAND AT TENNESSEE

YEAR	RECORD	BOWL
1926	8–1	
1927	8–0–1	
1928	9–0–1	
1929	9–0–1	
1930	9–1	
1931	9–0–1	
1932	9–0–1	
1933	7–3	
1934	8–2	
1936	6–2–2	
1937	6–3–1	
1938	11–0	Orange
1939	10–1	Rose
1940	10–1	Sugar
1946	9–2	Orange
1947	5–5	
1948	4–4–2	
1949	7–2–1	
1950	11–1	Cotton
1951	10–1	Sugar
1952	8–2–1	
Total	173–31–12	

right, commented on Neyland's philosophy. "If Neyland could score a touchdown against you, he had you beat," Hickman said. "If he could score two, he had you in a rout."

The General proved to be one of the game's great innovators. He developed a list of guiding principles and maxims firmly rooted in football's fundamentals and truths, influencing no lesser authorities than Paul "Bear" Bryant (who never beat Neyland), Knute Rockne, Wallace Wade, Bobby Dodd and countless others. More than 40 years after his death, the Volunteers still recite his maxims before every game. Neyland pioneered the use of press-box-to-bench telephones, analysis of game film for coaching purposes, lightweight silk football pants and tear-away jerseys.

Born in Greenville, Texas, Neyland established a pride in Tennessee football that continues unabated. As Hickman once told a group of Texans, "The State of Tennessee gave you Sam Houston and Davy Crockett; you gave us Bob Neyland. Now the score is even."

Coach Neyland's legendary 7 Maxims of Football were written decades ago but are timeless bits of wisdom that still apply to Tennessee football today:

1. *The team that makes the fewest mistakes will win.*

2. *Play for and make the breaks, and when one comes your way—SCORE.*

3. *If at first the game—or the breaks—go against you, don't let up...put on more steam.*

4. *Protect our kickers, our quarterback, our lead and our ball game.*

5. *Ball, oskie, cover, block, cut and slice, pursue and gang tackle...for this is the WINNING EDGE.*

6. *Press the kicking game. Here is where the breaks are made.*

7. *Carry the fight to our opponent and keep it there for 60 minutes.*

"I'm myself and I wouldn't pretend to be anyone else. The players know I'm prepared, I'm intense."

—TENNESSEE COACH PHILLIP FULMER

Phillip Fulmer

It began with the stock phrase heard at hiring press conferences around the nation. "I think we can take it to another level," Phillip Fulmer said when he was hired in November 1992, a pledge not necessarily notable in the annals of great oratory. Some poor soul whose mouth overreaches his ability says that very thing every year with the bright lights on and the cameras rolling. Most people making such a proclamation end up with a U-Haul in their driveway and a contract buyout in their hand in a few years. But Fulmer has proven he's not most people.

Fourteen years later, the road that runs in front of venerable Neyland Stadium bears his name. Fulmer's successful run includes a consensus national championship (1998), two

SEC championships (1997 and 1998), six SEC division titles and an impressive 128–37 (.776) worksheet.

The dean of SEC coaches owns a record of 95–30 in SEC play during the last 10 years, the best mark in the conference. No active coach with at least a decade of Division I-A experience can boast a better winning percentage than Fulmer's .776. Only five other coaches in the history of college football—legends George Woodruff, Barry Switzer, Tom Osborne, Bud Wilkinson and Amos Alonzo Stagg—reached 100 career victories fasten than Fulmer did.

Fulmer made his first mark on the Vol program as an offensive guard, helping pave the way for UT's 30–5 record from 1969 to 1971. Detail-oriented and organized, Fulmer has crafted a mobile and punishing defense and shares General Neyland's belief in the importance of the kicking game. Yet Fulmer's passion can be found on offense, preferring a balanced attack in which a bruising running game sets up a dangerous passing attack.

Fulmer excels in recruiting, showing his warmth for his players without making fool-hardy promises. His recruiting prowess is fortunate because, unlike Rose Bowl partici-pants Texas and USC, the Vols would not be in contention having to rely solely on home-grown talent.

Once Fulmer's gifted recruits arrive on the Hill, he develops them into coveted NFL players. Tennessee's NFL pipeline has swelled into a torrent on Fulmer's watch. Since 1994,

Tennessee has ranked first in the SEC and second nationally, with 75 players drafted. Fulmer has churned out millionaires faster than UT's nationally acclaimed business school has.

His 5–1 record in overtime games is a microcosm of the Fulmer way. When the game stands even, fatigue threatens bravery and winning depends on execution, the eyes of the Volunteer nation turn to the capable Fulmer. After spending 32 of his 56 years involved in Tennessee football as a player or coach, the Winchester native has become part of the fabric of the Volunteer State. Casting a long shadow on the sideline with the bill of his cap shielding intense eyes, Fulmer has indeed reached another level and has no intention of stopping his ascent of Rocky Top.

FULMER AT TENNESSEE

YEAR	RECORD	BOWL
1992	4–0	Hall of Fame
1993	10–2	Citrus
1994	8–4	Gator
1995	11–1	Citrus
1996	10–2	Citrus
1997	11–2	Orange
1998	13–0	Fiesta
1999	9–3	Fiesta
2000	8–4	Cotton
2001	11–2	Citrus
2002	8–5	Peach
2003	10–3	Peach
2004	10–3	Cotton
2005	5–6	
Total	128–37	

Tennessee was both lucky and good in 1998. Clint Stoerner's fumble led to a stunning 28–24 win over Arkansas, a key moment in the march to the national championship.

The 1914 Volunteers

VOLUNTEER SUPERLATIVES

Choosing the greatest teams, players and moments in Tennessee football history is like choosing your favorite grandchild. It's nearly impossible to single out one, or even to choose several; you love them all, and all of them have given you something special. But we've tried to pick the best of the best.

——— The Great Teams ———

The 1951 and 1998 national championship teams certainly weren't the only great teams in Vol history. Here's a quick sampling of some of the other great units to grace the Hill.

1914 (9–0)

Had there been wire service polls in 1914, coach Zora Clevenger's 1914 Tennessee team might have been national champs. Prior to that season, UT had been winless against Vanderbilt in 12 tries, but the Vols pulled off a 16–14 win in Nashville that year on the way to a perfect 9–0 slate, outscoring their opponents by a total of 374–37. Tennessee captured its first championship in football that season, finishing atop the Southern Intercollegiate Athletic Association standings.

1916 (8-0-1)

John R. Bender took over as Tennessee coach in 1916 and finished the year undefeated, though a scoreless tie with Kentucky in the season finale marred the record. As a result, the SIAA title was awarded to Georgia Tech. A 16–6 win over Vanderbilt brought UT's record against its cross-state rival to 2–12–1.

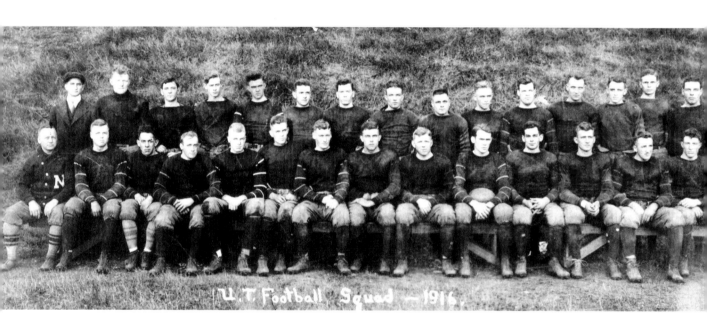

U.T. Football Squad — 1916.

1938 (11-0), 1939 (10-1), 1940 (10-1)

From 1938 through 1940, Bob Neyland's Tennessee teams enjoyed three straight perfect regular seasons. From midseason 1938 until midseason 1940, the Vols didn't surrender a regular-season point. The 1939 Tennessee team is the last in college football history to finish a regular season unscored upon. The record over those three years, counting bowl games: 31–2.

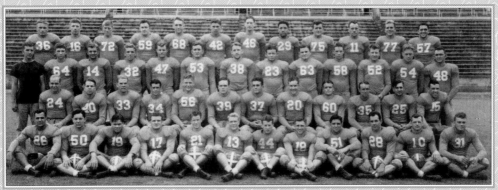

1938 Volunteers

**The 1939 starting backfield: Bob Foxx, Leonard Coffman,
George Cafego and Sam Bartholomew**

1940 Volunteers

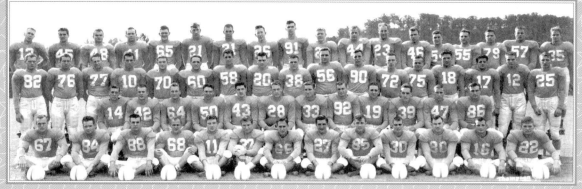

1950 Volunteers

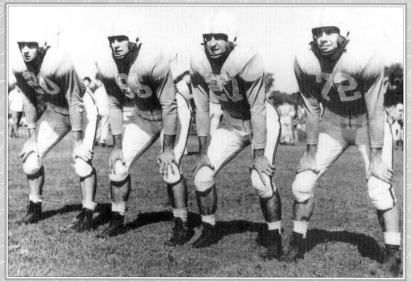

**The 1951 championship backfield: Bert Rechichar,
Andy Kozar, Hank Lauricella and Jimmy Hahn**

1951 Volunteers

1950 (11–1)

The Big Orange posted a 10–1 regular-season mark in 1950, dropping only Game 2 to Mississippi State. The biggest win of the year was a 7–0 decision over Bear Bryant's undefeated and top-ranked Kentucky team, which featured SEC Player of the Year Babe Parilli at quarterback on Nov. 25. The Vols went on to upset Texas 20–14 in the Cotton Bowl, keyed by a scintillating 75-yard run by Hank Lauricella. Two of the three teams ranked ahead of Tennessee—Oklahoma and Texas—lost their Bowl games, and second-ranked Army had lost to Navy on December 2. But the polls were closed.

1951 (10–1)

Tennessee's first consensus national championship came in the second-to-last year of Bob Neyland's coaching tenure. The 1951 Vols featured tailback Hank Lauricella, who finished second in that year's Heisman voting, and Doug Atkins, arguably the greatest defensive end who ever played the game. UT outscored its opponents 386–116 and finished the regular season 10–0 before dropping the Sugar Bowl to Maryland 28–13.

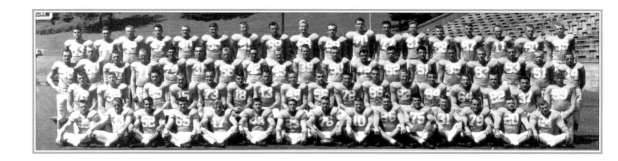

1956 (10–1)

With former Vol end and Hall of Fame coach Bowden Wyatt in his second season at the helm in Knoxville, Tennessee won the 1956 SEC Championship with a 10–0 regular-season record before dropping the Sugar Bowl to Baylor 13–7. The Vols' 6–0 win over Georgia Tech that year is an all-time college football classic. Tailback Johnny Majors finished second in the Heisman voting, and Tennessee finished second nationally in the final rankings.

1967 (9–2)

The 1967 Volunteers, with All-Americans Bob Johnson at center and Richmond Flowers at wingback, won the SEC and a share of the national championship. In between losses to UCLA and Heisman Trophy winner Gary Beban in the opener and to third-ranked Oklahoma in the Orange Bowl, the Vols were perfect. The highlight of the season was a 23–14 win at Alabama, which ended a six-year string of futility against the Tide.

1970 (11-1)

The Volunteers finished with a fourth-place national ranking in 1970, Bill Battle's inaugural season as head coach. The only smudge on the record was a three-point loss to Auburn in Game 2. Guard Chip Kell, defensive back Bobby Majors and linebacker Jackie Walker were All-Americans. The season was capped by a 34–10 rout of Air Force in the Sugar Bowl.

1989 (11-1)

The Vols won the second of coach Johnny Majors' three SEC Championships and ranked fifth in the final wire service polls with an 11–1 campaign in 1989. The only setback was a 47–30 shootout at Alabama. Antone Davis and All-American Eric Still were the most dominating guard duo in Knoxville since Bob Suffridge and Ed Molinski in the glory years of 1938–1940. Chuck Webb rushed for 1,236 yards at just under six per carry and added 250 rushing yards in a 31–27 Cotton Bowl victory over Southwest Conference champion Arkansas.

1998 (13–0)

Tennessee posted its second consensus national championship, and sixth overall, in 1998. Tee Martin took over for the graduated Peyton Manning at quarterback and led his team to the promised land. Tailback Jamal Lewis was lost for the season with a knee injury in Game 4, but Travis Henry answered the challenge and finished the season just 30 yards shy of a 1,000-yard rushing campaign. Wide receiver Peerless Price contributed 61 pass receptions to the cause. Linebackers Al Wilson and Raynoch Thompson cemented the defense, with place-kicker Jeff Hall becoming the SEC's all-time leading scorer. It took three fourth-quarter rallies to finish the regular season unscathed,

but these Vols were on a mission. After a resounding 23–16 victory over Florida State in the Fiesta Bowl, Tennessee stood at 13–0 as the undisputed national champion.

Travis Stephens holds the single-season rushing record at Tennessee.

Tennessee put an emphatic exclamation point on the 2001 season with a dominating win over Michigan.

"The last time we played a team as good as Tennessee—*it's been a while."*—MICHIGAN COACH LLOYD CARR FOLLOWING HIS TEAM'S 45–17 WHIPPING BY TENNESSEE IN THE 2002 CITRUS BOWL

2001 (11–2)

The 2001 Tennessee Vols came within half a game of playing for the national championship, falling to LSU in the SEC Championship Game. Instead, UT closed the season with one of the most impressive bowl victories in school history, trouncing Michigan 45–17 in the Citrus Bowl behind Casey Clausen's 26-of-34, 393-yard, three TD passing performance.

Indeed, it was one of the most prolific offensive squads to wear Orange and White, as future NFL receivers Donte Stallworth and Kelley Washington flanked future NFL Pro Bowl tight end Jason Witten. Travis Stephens, a speedy jitterbug back, provided an explosive burst out of the backfield.

Defensively, twin towers John Henderson and Albert Haynesworth thwarted the run from their tackle positions, and the tireless Will Overstreet provided a blind-side rush. Kevin Burnett ranked as one of the fiercest hitters in the nation in the linebacking corps, sidelining no fewer than three QBs during a season that included triumphs at Alabama (35–24), Notre Dame (28–18) and Florida (34–32).

The Greatest Games

TENNESSEE 15, ALABAMA 13
OCTOBER 20, 1928

Tennessee and Alabama hadn't played each other for 14 years, and the Crimson Tide had won eight of the previous 11 meetings. But this was the first game with Bob Neyland at the helm for the Volunteers. Neyland's first two teams had posted records of 8–1 and 8–0–1, an accomplishment scarcely known outside of Knoxville. The Volunteers needed a win over somebody big, and nobody was bigger than Alabama, which was coming off consecutive Rose Bowl trips under coach Wallace Wade. Tennessee sophomore halfback Gene McEver's 98-yard touchdown on the opening kickoff opened the festivities, and the Vols won the game 15–13. The win focused national attention on Tennessee and its "Hack, Mack and Dodd" backfield of Buddy Hackman, McEver and Bobby Dodd.

TENNESSEE 17, OKLAHOMA 0
JANUARY 2, 1939

Tennessee finished the 1938 regular season 10–0 and ranked second in the nation behind TCU and Heisman Trophy winner Davey O'Brien. The Vols' first-ever bowl game—in the Orange Bowl against fourth-ranked Oklahoma—ensued. The Sooners were also 10–0 and had won their last 14 games. The game was billed as one of speed (Tennessee) versus power (Oklahoma). Speed won. It is remembered as one of the most vicious football games ever played. One journalist referred to the contest as the "Orange Brawl." Players were knocked out of the game with startling regularity. A block by Tennessee All-American George Cafego finished OU All-American Waddy Young for the day. UT center Joe Little was ejected from the game for retaliating after a Sooner cheap shot. Touchdowns by Bob Foxx and Babe Wood, a Bowden Wyatt field goal, and a shutout by a typically impenetrable Neyland defense, rendered a final tally of 17–0.

(Above) Abe Shires, Bob Suffridge, Bowden Wyatt, George Cafego and Babe Wood gather outside the Knoxville train station prior to departing for the 1939 Orange Bowl, where they would make history. Below: Buist Warren heads upfield in Tennessee's 17–0 Orange Bowl whitewash of Oklahoma.

TENNESSEE 7, KENTUCKY 0
NOVEMBER 25, 1950

Many observers felt the 1950 Tennessee team was superior to its 1951 national champions. After dropping Game 2 to Mississippi State, the 1950 Vols rolled over seven straight opponents before their matchup with Bear Bryant's undefeated, top-ranked Kentucky team. The Wildcats, led by Southeastern Conference MVP Babe Parilli at quarterback, had already clinched the SEC crown. The Vols weren't given much of a chance entering the contest, but their defense, spearheaded by Bill Pearman, Ted Daffer, Bud Sherrod and Doug Atkins, kept Parilli on the run most of the day. A 27-yard touchdown pass from Hank Lauricella to Bert Rechichar was all the scoring the Big Orange needed.

LAURICELLA 3 YDS PAST LINE OF SCRIMMAGE ON 75 YD RUN AGAINST TEXAS IN COTTON BOWL JANUARY 1ST 1951

HAHN HITS MENASCO

KOZAR TAKES OUT GEORGES

LYONS DELAYS McFADIN

MICHELS HEADS FOR DILLON

RECHICHAR AND KASETA FLATTEN DAVIS

CUNNINGHAM AVOIDS STROUD, FINALLY MAKES TACKLE 70 YARDS DOWN FIELD

GRUBLE LUNGES TOWARD OCHOA

TENNESSEE 20, TEXAS 14
JANUARY 1, 1951

Had the final polls been taken after the post-season in 1950, as they are today, Tennessee would have been national champion. Neyland's Vols, 10–1 and ranked fourth nationally, traveled to Dallas to take on the 9–1, third-ranked Texas Longhorns in the Cotton Bowl on New Year's Day, 1951. The Volunteers scored first on a short pass from Herky Payne to John Gruble. The score was set up by a memorable 75-yard run by All-American Hank Lauricella. The Horns stormed back to lead 14–7 at intermission, but the Vols owned the second half. Neyland's troops, using the single wing formation that had been ditched by all but one or two other teams in favor of the T formation, stormed back for 13 fourth-quarter points on a pair of touchdown plunges by fullback Andy Kozar. Tennessee's speed won over Texas' bulk to the tune of a 20–14 final score. With top-ranked Oklahoma falling to Kentucky in the Sugar Bowl that same day, a post-bowl poll would have crowned Tennessee champion.

Known, simply, as "the Stop." Heisman winner Billy Cannon is stopped just short of the end zone on a two-point conversion in Tennessee's epic 14–13 upset of LSU.

TENNESSEE 6, GEORGIA TECH 0
NOVEMBER 10, 1956

In 1956, Bowden Wyatt enjoyed the best campaign of his eight-year coaching regime in Knoxville. Tennessee and then-SEC foe Georgia Tech, coached by former UT Vol Bobby Dodd, were each 6–0 entering their classic matchup. Wyatt and Dodd had both trained as players under Neyland, and now they coached the two finest teams in the Southeastern Conference. A pair of third-quarter passes from Johnny Majors to Buddy Cruze set up the game's only score, a 1-yard plunge by Tommy Bronson. The Vols held on for the win in what was to be Tech's only loss of the season.

TENNESSEE 14, LSU 13
NOVEMBER 7, 1959

In 1959, LSU was the defending national champion, with Paul Dietzel as coach and Heisman Trophy winner Billy Cannon as its star halfback. The Bayou Bengals brought a 19-game winning streak and number-one ranking into Knoxville on November 7 to face the 4–1–1 Vols. Cannon and Johnny Robinson ran wild in the first half for LSU, but the Tigers could only manage to squeeze out 7 points by halftime. In the third period, Tennessee's Jim Cartwright intercepted a Warren Rabb pass and returned it 59 yards for a game-tying touchdown. The Vols took a 14–7 lead on a 14-yard Neyle Solle run. A fumbled punt at the 2-yard line led to LSU's final touchdown and brought the score to 14–13. But Cannon was stopped short on the 2-point conversion try in one of the greatest moments in Tennessee football history, preserving the huge upset win.

It was a magical night in New Orleans. Quarterback Daryl Dickey led a stunning 35–7 rout of Miami in the Sugar Bowl, unleashing a wild Bourbon Street celebration.

TENNESSEE 35, MIAMI 7
JANUARY 1, 1986

Miami finished the 1985 regular season on a 10-game winning streak, having not lost since dropping its opener to Florida 35–23. Coach Jimmy Johnson brought his Hurricanes into the Sugar Bowl to face Johnny Majors' SEC Champion Tennessee squad. The 'Canes took a 7–0 lead on an 18-yard pass from Vinny Testaverde to Michael Irvin to end the first quarter, but after that it was all UT. A 6-yard touchdown pass from Daryl Dickey to Jeff

Smith in the second quarter knotted the score at 7–7 and sent the game spiraling out of Miami's control. The Vols led 14–7 at the half, tacked on two more TDs in the third period, including a 60-yard punt return by Jeff Powell, and another in the fourth. The defense produced seven sacks and six turnovers, sending the highly partisan crowd into a frenzy that spilled onto Bourbon Street. The final tally: Tennessee 35, Miami 7. It was the resounding exclamation point on one of the truly magical seasons in Tennessee history.

A key moment in Tennessee's greatest comeback win: Floyd Miley scoops up a blocked field goal and races toward the end zone just before halftime to cut Notre Dame's lead to 31–14. The rest is Volunteer history.

TENNESSEE 35, NOTRE DAME 34
NOVEMBER 9, 1991

It was the greatest come-from-behind win in Tennessee history and the greatest comeback ever at Notre Dame Stadium. On November 9, 1991, at South Bend, Notre Dame jumped out to a 21–0 first-quarter lead and led 31–7 in the second quarter. Just before halftime, Darryl Hardy blocked a field goal attempt by ND's Craig Hentrich. Floyd Miley scooped up the ball and took off on an 85-yard touchdown jaunt to bring the score to 31–14 at intermission. The Volunteers scored three TDs in the second half, including two by Aaron Hayden, to take the lead 35–34. Irish walk-on kicker Rob Leonard, subbing for an injured Hentrich, came in for a 27-yard field goal as time expired, but Jeremy Lincoln blocked the attempt and the Vols came away winners.

One of the wildest, most satisfying celebrations Knoxville has ever seen followed Tennessee's 20–17 win over nemesis Steve Spurrier and Florida in 1998's championship season.

TENNESSEE 20, FLORIDA 17
SEPTEMBER 19, 1998

Tennessee's 34–33 win over Syracuse in the 1998 season opener could qualify for greatest-game status, but it was the Vols' next game, two weeks later against Florida, that fans remember most fondly. After a Florida field goal, Shawn Bryson scored on a 57-yard run for a 7–3 Tennessee lead in the first quarter. The first half ended in a 10–10 deadlock. After three quarters the score was knotted at 17, and the final period was scoreless. Jeff Hall kicked a 41-yard field goal in the first-ever overtime period for both schools, and UT led 20–17. Jeff Chandler came up empty on his 32-yard attempt to end the Gators' overtime posses-sion, and the Vols were off and running to a national title. Deon Grant's fourth-quarter interception and linebacker Al Wilson's nine tackles and school-record three forced fumbles were keys to the win. And the Neyland Stadium goal-post enjoyed a late-night parade through the strip as Knoxville celebrated like never before.

TENNESSEE 34, FLORIDA 32
DECEMBER 1, 2001

Steve Spurrier appeared to have the Vols right where he wanted them in the final moments, but UT reserve defensive back Buck Fitzgerald blanketed star receiver Jabar Gaffney on a 2-point conversion pass attempt from Rex Grossman, and helped to secure a 34–32 victory.

The Gators were on their heels all game long. A Vols receiving corps that included Donte Stallworth, Kelley Washington and tight end Jason Witten left Florida in defensive sets that were susceptible to the run, and Travis Stephens took full advantage with a 19-carry, 226-yard, two-TD performance.

TENNESSEE 51, ALABAMA 43
(5 OT)
OCTOBER 25, 2003

The Vols' defense stepped up at the end of regulation, stopping the Tide on three consecutive plays when all Alabama needed was 2 yards to run out the clock. Once with the ball, Casey Clausen orchestrated an 86-yard touchdown drive in the final two minutes to tie the game at 20–20 and send the battle into overtime.

From the final drive of regulation to the end of the fifth overtime, Clausen was at his best, going 10-for-17 for 146 yards and four touchdowns, and rushing for the game-winner. Clausen also completed a fourth-and-19 pass to C.J. Fayton in overtime to keep the game alive.

"There's not a tougher-minded quarterback in the country than Casey Clausen," UT coach Phillip Fulmer said. "He's as tough physically and mentally as I've ever been around." The win boosted Clausen's mark to 3–0 in overtime games, 12–1 on the road and gave him his six fourth-quarter comeback win.

Florida quarterback Rex Grossman (8) is sacked by Tennessee's John Henderson (98) during the third quarter on Saturday, December 1, 2001 in Gainesville, Florida.

TENNESSEE 10, MIAMI 6
NOVEMBER 8, 2003

A near-scuffle in the pregame warm-ups set the tone for one of the hardest-hitting games in Tennessee history as the Vols battled a Hurricanes team riding a 26-game home win streak.

"This game was about respect," said UT linebacker Kevin Burnett, whose team certainly earned it by holding Miami without a touchdown in the Orange Bowl for the first time in 19 years. For all the big plays, which included Corey Campbell's head-splitting shot on 'Canes All-America tight end Kellen Winslow—which later led to Winslow's infamous locker room "soldier" tirade—the biggest play of all came at the UT 9-yard line. There

free safety Mark Jones pressured Brock Berlin into an errant pass that strong safety Gibril Wilson picked off to secure the win. It was one of four turnovers the Vols forced on that day.

Tennessee managed just one touchdown drive, a 15-play 73-yarder that featured one of the biggest play-call gambles of Phillip Fulmer's career. Facing a fourth-and-goal at the 'Canes' 2-yard line, there was time for just one more play. Fulmer shocked Miami and the Vol Nation by abandoning his conservative ways, eschewing a field goal attempt and calling an end-around to Derrick Tinsley, of all things. Tinsley beat Miami All-America safety Sean Taylor to the corner of the end zone to provide all the scoring Tennessee needed in its biggest win of the new millennium.

Vols coach Phillip Fulmer made one of the gutsiest calls of his renowned career to beat Miami in Tennessee's clash with the host Hurricanes.

TENNESSEE 30, LSU 27
SEPTEMBER 26, 2005

The brightest moment of the otherwise down-trodden 5–6 2005 season was provided by Rick Clausen, who returned to the school he transferred from and made magic with a storybook comeback finish amid curious circumstances.

Hurricanes Katrina and Rita forced the game to be moved back to Monday night at Tiger Stadium, and a lack of hotel rooms forced the Vols to fly in the day of the game.

Early on, the delay appeared to benefit LSU, as the Tigers jumped out to a 21–0 lead by jumping on sophomore Erik Ainge, who was clearly not having his best night.

The Tigers were up 24–7 entering the fourth quarter before Clausen gave LSU fans reasons to wonder how they'd ever let him get away. Clausen led Tennessee on a 13-play, 75-yard drive that he capped with a 1-yard QB sneak to draw the Volunteers within 10.

Cornerback Jonathan Hefney provided the next big life on LSU's ensuing drive, stepping in front of a JaMarcus Russell pass and returning it 24 yards to the Tigers' 2-yard line. Tailback Gerald Riggs scored on a 2-yard run, and suddenly it was 24–21 and the Volunteers were back in a game that had appeared hopeless just one hour earlier.

The Tennessee defense held firm, forcing a punt, and a 22-yard Riggs run set up James Wilhoit's game-tying 28-yard field goal.

LSU drew first blood in overtime with a field goal, but Riggs and the Volunteers weren't to be denied. Riggs caught a 10-yard pass and rushed for 14 yards on a carry. Finally, Riggs bulled through Tiger defenders for a 1-yard game-winning touchdown that left the hurricane-ravaged state of Louisiana in further shock.

Who would have believed that the same Rick Clausen who wasn't good enough to start for the Bayou Bengals three years earlier could return with a 21-of-32, 196-yard passing performance?

The Great Moments

PUNT, BEATTIE, PUNT

The 1932 Tennessee-Alabama game was the scene of the greatest punting duel in college football history. The backdrop was rainy, mud-soaked Legion Field in Birmingham. Tennessee coach Bob Neyland and Alabama coach Frank Thomas both decided to play conservatively and await the other team's mistakes. Vol half-back Beattie Feathers averaged 48 yards on 21 punts. His Crimson-clad counterpart, fullback Johnny Cain, punted 19 times at 43 yards per boot. 'Bama blinked first. Punting from his own end zone in the fourth quarter, Cain had to leap for a high pass from center. His hurried kick traveled only to the Tide 12-yard line. Three plays later, Feathers slashed into the end zone for the game's only touchdown, and Tennessee won 7–3.

JOHNNY BUTLER PAST LINE OF SCRIMMAGE ON 56 YD. RUN AGAINST ALABAMA. SHIELDS-WATKINS FIELD — OCTOBER 21, 1939

BUTLER'S RUN

The most memorable play ever in Neyland Stadium, known at the time as Shields-Watkins Field, was achieved by a sophomore second-string halfback. In the 1939 Alabama game, Johnny "Blood" Butler eluded every player on the Alabama defense in a twisting, darting, 56-yard touchdown run. They all had a shot at him, but no one laid a hand on him. Legendary sportswriter Grantland Rice, in attendance in the press box that day, termed Butler's run the greatest he had ever seen. And oh, by the way, the Tennessee Volunteers won 21–0.

THE ARTFUL DODGER

Condredge Holloway's artistic escape acts became legendary during the little quarterback's tenure at Tennessee and resulted in some memorable victories. But the most remarkable performance by the man they called the Artful Dodger may have come in a game the Volunteers didn't win. In the 1974 season opener against UCLA, Holloway led Tennessee to a 10–0 first-quarter lead before injuring his shoulder. Holloway was rushed to a nearby hospital for X-rays, which proved negative. Returning to Neyland Stadium to deafening roars, Holloway reentered the game over the objections of coach Bill Battle. With Tennessee facing a 17–10 deficit, the Huntsville Houdini rallied the Vols to a tying touchdown, leaping over defenders into the end zone at the end of a 12-yard fourth-quarter run.

"I'M GOING TO STAY..."

When Peyton Manning walked to the podium for a press conference in March 1997, many people were prepared for the worst. Manning had rewritten the Tennessee record books during his three years as the unofficial president of Vol Nation, and the riches of professional football that were seemingly his birthright beckoned him to leave The Hill after his junior season.

But Manning, the type of kid for whom the phrase *student-athlete* was seemingly coined, had other ideas. The following nine-word statement thrilled fans all across Rocky Top and stunned others who were certain he was leaving:

"I'm going to stay at the University of Tennessee."

The packed house erupted as fellow players, media, athletic department officials, friends and family reveled in the news. "I've had an incredible experience at the University of Tennessee with all the people I've met, learned from and become friends with here," Manning explained. "College football has been great to me, so have the people, and the coaches and players I've played with the past three years. I wanted to come back and be a college student one more year and enjoy the entire experience."

Said coach Phillip Fulmer: "Today we are blessed with the ultimate return of loyalty and commitment...Peyton's decision makes a huge statement, I think, for Peyton Manning and his character, putting team and program and alumni and fans and friends and teammates ahead of immediate financial gains and the limelight of the National Football League."

A moment that thrilled Tennessee fans everywhere: "I'm going to stay at the University of Tennessee."

THE RIVALRIES

Welcome to your poor man's therapy session. It's time to find your happy place, Tennessee football fans. Close your eyes. Picture a sun-kissed day beside the Tennessee River with 107,000 of your closest friends toasting a fruitful fall under an azure sky.

Take a deep breath. Relax. Your Volunteers will win this one easily. The scoreboard reads: Tennessee 45, _____ 0.

Fellow Volunteers, it's all about how you choose to fill in the blank. If you had to pick just one, which rival deserves the 45-0 drubbing the most?

Haywood Harris, athletics department historian and resident living legend, knows as much about Tennessee football tradition as anyone. "You're not supposed to like your rivals," Harris said. "You may like the people, but you don't like their goal because their goal is to beat you."

Rivalries in Tennessee football remain a big deal, surviving and thriving long after their architects have taken to drawing up plays in the clouds on the great gridiron in the sky. Imagine a football schedule without Florida, Georgia, Alabama, Vanderbilt and Kentucky appearing. It would be like getting water when you were promised watermelon—maybe enough to sustain you but not nearly as sweet.

"You have rivalries, archrivalries and hallowed rivalries," Harris said. "Anyone you play is a rival because they're trying to beat you. I put Florida and Georgia into the archrival category. Florida hasn't been a great rivalry for that long a time. Hallowed rivalries are reserved for Alabama, Kentucky and Vanderbilt."

What makes a great rivalry? That's one of the few football questions on which Neyland failed to provide guidance in his timeless maxims.

Certainly geography plays a role in the formation of Harris' hallowed rivalries. Border battles fit the bill, the tension ramped up all the more because proximity promoted regular contact with *them*. Similarly, border battles help ensure a faithful following to the road games.

Harris relates a story about the allure of the Kentucky rivalry. In 1947 Kentucky ranked as one of Tennessee's fiercest football rivals. Many of the games were tight, and once in a great while, Kentucky would sneak up and ruin the Vols' chances at an esteemed bowl, which were much more scarce in that day.

This rivalry prompted four UT freshmen—Harris, future Voice of the Vols John Ward, James Dunford and George Kirby—to pile in an old Plymouth and head north for the 1947 edition of the Tennessee-Kentucky rivalry on a cold Friday night. When the quartet hit Richmond, Kentucky, the car's headlights died, putting them in a tight spot. With Harris driving through sleet and snow, a frozen Ward rode the rest of the trip out on the running board, clutching a flashlight to guide the way. No Interstate 75 existed at the time, which Harris said made the improvisation safer and warmer. "We couldn't go as fast, so it was safer and warmer for him on the running board," Harris said. Now we know why Ward always broadcast with a blue towel draped around his neck. He never thawed out.

The foursome finally arrived safely in Lexington that night and was rewarded with a 13–6 Tennessee victory the next day. Harris' belief was that because the game involved a hallowed rival, all the trouble was worth it, though perhaps Ward begged to differ.

Perhaps the passion of Southern football survives as a vestige of dueling frontiersmen. Honor must be defended at all costs.

There are no ties (anymore). One team will fall wounded. The other notches his pistol and swaggers into the autumn sunset. The high-stakes nature is exacerbated by the fact that, unlike most other collegiate sports, a football rivalry game occurs only once a year unless the parties meet for a rematch in the SEC championship game.

Besides bringing a different feel, a rivalry is evident in tangible signs as well. Ticket prices spiral to incredible heights as an impromptu economics course plays out on the sidewalks of campus. Tailgate menus become more elabo-rate and the invitation lists grow when a rival hits town. In the event of a win, a river of revelers flows in torrents down the Cumberland Avenue Strip. If the forces of darkness manage to defeat the home team, there may be a little more room in the pew at church Sunday morning.

The venerable SEC creates a veritable petri dish for the cultivation of rivalries. It's been said that if you like anyone in your confer-ence, then you don't have a very good conference. Peel back enough seasons and you can find a grudge match with every school in the conference in one sport or another. Thus, the Tennessee gridders are duty-bound to avenge their Volunteer ancestors and deliver a thumping on the gridiron. And so it grows.

———— Tennessee vs. Florida ————

While the historian Harris may only rate Florida as an archrival ranking just in the middle of his blood-boiling scale, no small portion of the Vol Nation considers the boys from old Florida public enemy number one. Surely the very foundation of the Smokies would quake and Neyland Stadium would slide into the Tennessee River if the Gators were omitted from the Vols' current list of white-hot rivalries.

The Tennessee-Florida rivalry formed differently than the others. The two schools didn't begin meeting annually until 1990. While other factors primed this tinderbox, the 1992 split of the SEC into Eastern and Western divisions provided the big bang. When judged against other great graybeard Southern rivalries, the Tennessee-Florida hostility rates but a teenager. But the passion and temper of the teenager packs a short fuse, and the SEC siblings continue their stormy adolescence.

Part of the spirited feeling arises from the fact that Tennesseans and the rest of the South regard the residents of the Sunshine State as impostors—a little more mall than y'all. Such members of that school of thought question Florida's spiritual association with the other football kings of Dixie.

It's small wonder the rivalry became supercharged in such a short period of time. We should all be grateful to Georgia for the separation. Florida as a border battle could have been mighty ugly.

Even though the schools met only occasionally in the early years, a fundamental distrust fertilized the Tennessee-Florida rivalry early, a true hallmark of a great rivalry.

Above all others on the Volunteer hit list, Tennessee-Florida has offered a home sweet home to the conspiracy theorists of both parties. The schools have swapped players, coaches and administrators at the highest levels over the years. These interactions have caused a tangled web of conspiracy theories.

It didn't take long for the craziness to ensue. In 1928, just the third game of the

series, Tennessee won a 13–12 squeaker. In the first conspiracy theory of the series, but certainly not the last, the Florida coaches complained that the Tennessee groundskeepers had "watered" the field.

Bob Woodruff, who played under Neyland at Tennessee, served as Florida's head coach before returning to Tennessee to build an impressive all-around program as athletics director. Doug Dickey ranked as one of Woodruff's prized quarterbacks during his coaching career at Florida. The great coaching swap at the end of the 1969 sent Knoxville's conspiracy hounds on a hot trail, prompting barking that continues in some doghouses to this day. Dickey served admirably as head coach at Tennessee from 1964 to 1969. Dickey brought his Vols into the Gator Bowl to face his alma mater and cap the 1969 season. With rumors rampant that Dickey would replace Florida coach Ray Graves, who interestingly enough played under Neyland at Tennessee, the Gators defeated the Vols 14–13. Despite the fact that it wasn't in Dickey's self-interest to lose the game, a small contingent of Tennessee supporters never forgave him. Later, Dickey followed his old coach Woodruff in a charmed tenure as Vol athletics director.

The series took an ominous turn when Johnson City, Tennessee, native Steve Spurrier spurned the Volunteers and signed with Florida. Though Spurrier never played against his homeland Vols, the Benedict Arnold shadow had fallen upon him. Truth be known, as a quarterback, Florida's style of play fit Spurrier much better than Tennessee's at the time. Spurrier was rewarded with the Heisman Trophy in 1966. Spurrier's capture of the Heisman rankled Tennessee, as the Vols, despite their certified status as one of college football's greatest programs, have been stiff-armed by the elusive trophy.

Later, as Gator head coach, Spurrier drove the rivalry to new heights with his coaching ability and needling antics. His Fun 'n' Gun offense and loquacious manner drove the rest of the conference crazy. He never met a microphone he didn't like, and stadium

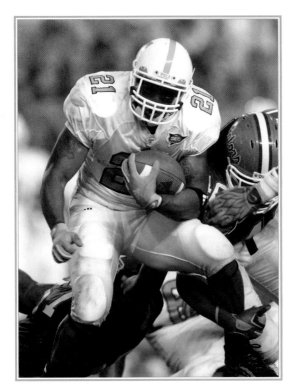

maintenance workers around the conference stayed busy replacing overworked light bulbs in the scoreboard. A man doesn't earn the nicknames "Saint Steve," "Coach Superior" and "Evil Genius" without a healthy dose of ability and a colorful personality.

Ill winds blew as Florida was stripped of its 1984 SEC football title, its first in program history, because of significant NCAA violations. The Gators defeated the Vols that year, and it doesn't take a clairvoyant to figure out how Tennessee voted on the issue at the SEC

meetings. Making matters worse for Florida, the Gators topped the Vols again in 1985 on their way to what would have been another SEC title. However, Tennessee took the hardware while Florida continued its probation purgatory.

The mutual distrust intensified in 1991 when Jack Sells, a fired Tennessee assistant, faxed portions of Tennessee's playbook to Ron Zook, a Florida assistant at the time. Zook served as Tennessee's defensive backs coach from 1984 to 1986 and later as Florida's head coach after Spurrier bolted for the NFL's Washington Redskins. Florida won the 1991 battle of the fax faux pas 35–18.

The 1992 game only magnified the importance of the annual September affair. In 1992 the SEC split into Eastern and Western divisions whose champions would meet at the end of the regular season in the SEC championship game for a coveted slot in the Sugar Bowl or often an inside track to the national championship game. With both teams annually in the

SEC East turf war, the early season game crowns one team a front-runner and the other behind the eight ball in the race to the division title. Tennessee won the 1992 game 31–14 under interim head coach Phillip Fulmer.

Several of Tennessee's most memorable wins of the last decade were nabbed against Florida. Vol fans still treasure the 1998 "pandemonium reigns" overtime game to keep alive the dream season. Tennesseans still remember tailback Travis Stephens, the little engine that could, steamrolling favored Florida to the tune of 226 rushing yards in the rare December meeting between the rivals in 2001, Spurrier's curtain call in the series. Wilhoit's goat-to-hero transformation as the clock wound down in 2004 remains fresh in the conscience of a grateful Vol Nation.

No one knows when the next great chapter of this heated rivalry will be penned, but the wise words that Ben Byrd, the elder statesman of Knoxville sports journalists, wrote before the supercharged 1996 game still apply today. "Each team stands in the other's way," Byrd wrote. "There will be no championship for the losers. They will drink the bitter wine.

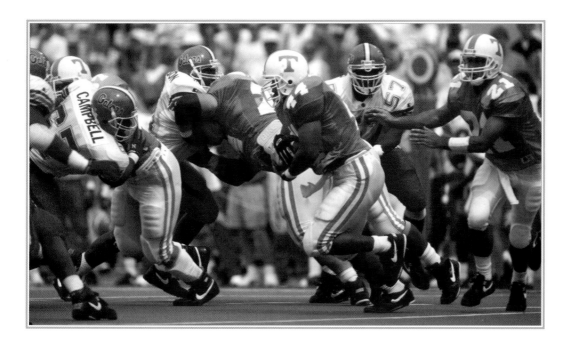

In a series of streaks, no streak-buster was more satisfying than Tennessee's 35–28 win over Alabama in 1982, Bear Bryant's last game in the series.

Tennessee vs. Alabama

The Alabama series stands as the antithesis of Tennessee's Florida rivalry. Tennessee-Alabama has always been a clean, hard-fought rivalry steeped in a mutual, if grudging, admiration. "This has been a class series between class people," Gus Manning, the longest-serving member of Tennessee's athletics department, said. Since 1901, the winner of the Tennessee-Alabama game enjoyed the inside track to the rightful claim as the kings of Dixie football.

Though not Tennessee's oldest rivalry, the Volunteers versus the Tide is almost biblical in its duration, scope and passion. Neyland begat Bowden Wyatt, who begat Dickey, who begat Johnny Majors, who begat Fulmer. Across the border, Wallace Wade begat Frank Thomas, who begat Paul "Bear" Bryant, who begat Gene Stallings. The caliber of the coaches involved—the architects of the rivalry—helped to make Tennessee-Alabama special in the annals of Southern football.

The third Saturday in October, or whenever *the* game is played that fall, ranks as a high, holy day in Southern football. The annual scrum is so legendary that even the forces of nature take part. The maples in all their autumn splendor cast their allegiance with brilliant votes of orange and crimson. The mere mention of Tennessee-Alabama evokes the aroma of cigar smoke and crumpled hickory leaves.

In the 1920s, the Volunteers weren't getting a great deal of national ink. In 1928, Neyland's bold move to schedule national power Alabama would give the national press reason to take note of the upstart Volunteers. Neyland became the nemesis of the Tide, running up a 12–5–2 record against the gentlemen from the Capstone.

In 1928, Neyland's Vols renewed the series in Tuscaloosa as heavy underdogs to Wade's Tide. However, the Vols wasted no time elbowing into the elite of Southern football as Gene "Wild Bull" McEver returned the opening kickoff 98 yards. Tennessee beat the pride of the Yellowhammer State 15–13, as Neyland

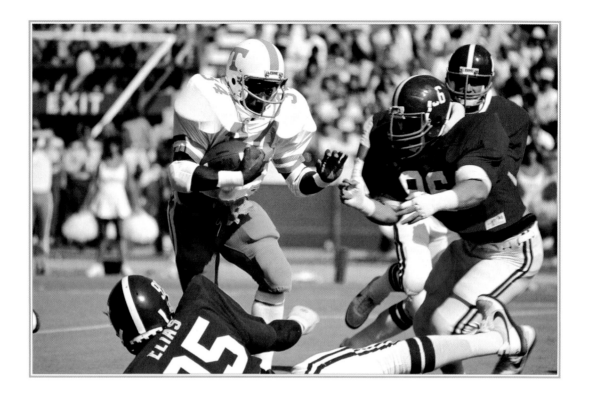

parted the Tide and the Vols followed him into national football prominence.

The Tennessee-Alabama rivalry has long been a series of streaks, with the Tide often stringing together the longer streak. The streaky nature of the series heightens the importance of winning because of the difficulty of breaking such a run. As a bragging point in the border battle, the streaks tend to take on a life of their own.

The Vols own three separate four-win streaks in the series and ripped off a program-best, seven-game streak against the Tide from 1995–2001 on Fulmer's watch. However, Alabama's streaks have often been longer, including a couple of seven-game runs and a painfully extended 11-game reign from 1971 to 1981. During the long droughts, it's almost enough to cause a Vol fan to pull a Rip Van Winkle hibernation. Just wake me when it's over.

The series has produced a bumper crop of heroes as collegiate careers were made in the rivalry. Merely great plays and moments were transformed into iconic images of Tennessee's proud history simply because they were authored in the Alabama series.

In 1932, with offenses mired in the muck and the rain still falling, both teams relied on their punters to change field position. Tennessee's Beattie Feathers punted 21 times for a 43-yard average. Alabama's Johnny Cain punted 19 times for a 48-yard average. The scoreboard showed the most important stat: Tennessee 7, Alabama 3.

Even early in the series, missing the game was not a decision made lightly. Bryant, who played in the 1935 Tennessee-Alabama game with a broken leg, told his Tide troops that you became a man in the Tennessee game.

Tennessee's Johnny Butler authored one of the most famous runs in school history with his 56-yard hopscotch against Alabama in 1939, his circuitous route winding like a copperhead. No less an authority than Grantland Rice, considered by many the finest sportswriter ever to put pen to paper, called it the greatest run he had ever seen.

The 1946 game offered an example of the rivalry at its finest and classiest. Tennessee

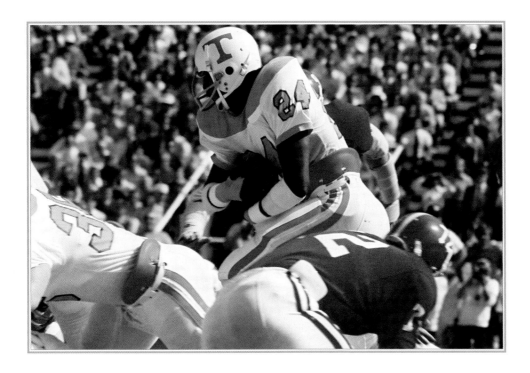

topped Alabama 12–0 after Harry Gilmer, the Tide's talented quarterback, was pummeled repeatedly by Tennessee's hard-charging Dick Huffman. But Gilmer understood the importance of the rivalry and courageously dragged himself up and back into the fray time and again. When Gilmer was finally pulled by his coaches late in the game, the crowd at Shields-Watkins Field gave him a standing ovation.

In 1982, The goal posts tumbled at Neyland Stadium as Tennessee turned back the Tide 35–28 after 11 consecutive losses. The game marked Bryant's curtain call in a series he helped make so special. Another iconic moment in the series was captured as Majors rode to midfield on the shoulders of his players to reach down and shake Bryant's hand as the man in the houndstooth hat made his last stroll across the checkerboard.

The 1985 edition of the rivalry loomed darkly. Tennessee quarterback Tony Robinson lay crumpled on Legion Field, his knee shredded. Enter backup Daryl Dickey, who ably guided the Vols to a 16–14 win. Alabama quarterback and current head coach Mike Shula had his aerial swatted and then intercepted by Tennessee's everyman hero Dale Jones. Jones' memorable defensive play inspired a painting, surely sharing treasured wall space with photos of weddings, graduations and family reunions in homes across the Volunteer State.

One of the most recent highlights of the series proved to be an audible one, as Tennessee players of the late 1990s took artistic liberties with Lynyrd Skynyrd's "Sweet Home Alabama," opting for "We Own Alabama."

The latest classic in a series full of them occurred in 2003. Tennessee prevailed 51–43 in a five-overtime thriller in Tuscaloosa. The score by quarters, all nine of them, looked like a line score from a fall classic in a different sport.

In recent years, the intensity of the rivalry has heightened and, some would say, changed for the worse. Alabama's travails with the NCAA landed the Tide on probation. The fact that Phillip Fulmer, among other coaches, was interviewed by the NCAA in the process revved up a litany of threats, flying in the face of the rivalry's character.

Admirers of the rivalry hope that the passage of time will snuff out the tomfoolery of the present and return the SEC brethren to a more amicable future.

The Future

No one's suggesting that Florida and Alabama will concede a yard to the Vols, as those rivalries continue to burn plenty hot. However, one doesn't have to look any farther than the SEC East to see the makings of new rivalries.

Though the Vols and the "Silver Britches" of Georgia have met in some donnybrooks before, head coach Mark Richt's resurrection of the Georgia program will likely offer plenty of grist for the SEC rival mill. Georgia's recent reversal of Tennessee's 1990s dominance of the series turned up the heat on this border battle. With all due respect to UGA, one can be assured that Fulmer awaits the next opportunity to return Smokey IX to top-dog status in the dog-eat-dog SEC.

Though South Carolina's football history pales in the shadow of other SEC giants, Spurrier's hiring adds instant octane to this rivalry. At Kentucky and Alabama, Bryant set the precedent for leading two schools into white-hot rivalries with the Volunteers. Spurrier possesses the ability and ego to pull off the same.

Until last November, most Vol fans would snicker at Harris' classification of Vanderbilt as a hallowed rival. Surely the Vols' most unlikely loss of the 2005 season will breathe new life into the ancient intrastate rivalry.

No one knows for sure which present rivalries will wax and wane and which new names will join Tennessee's hit list as the Vols march into the future. One matter is not up for debate: since 1891, the football Volunteers of Tennessee have shirked no challengers. The rewards have also run the gamut from black eyes and blue bruises to bronze trophies and golden rings. Tennesseans don't dodge anyone, taking on "anything, anywhere, anytime—bar nothing."

TALKIN' TENNESSEE FOOTBALL

"Mr. Speaker, I have often said that in my district, the colors orange and white are almost as patriotic as red, white and blue. That is because orange and white represents the official colors of the University of Tennessee and the Tennessee Volunteers football team, now the undisputed NCAA national football champion.

"Mr. Speaker, just a few short weeks ago the Tennessee Vols completed a perfect 13-0 season and earned their first national championship in 47 years.

"Mr. Speaker, I congratulate the newly crowned NCAA National Champion Tennessee Volunteers and everyone who has contributed to their perfect season. Go Vols!"

— EXCERPTS FROM REMARKS MADE BY TENNESSEE CONGRESSMAN
JOHN DUNCAN ON THE FLOOR OF THE UNITED STATES
HOUSE OF REPRESENTATIVES, JANUARY 19, 1999

"I'll be a Tennessee Volunteer *for the rest of my life."*
—PEYTON MANNING

"Peyton is the fastest thinker *I've ever been around. He has a computer for a mind, and he can bring that into use under center. He computes it all so fast."* —TENNESSEE OFFENSIVE COORDINATOR DAVID CUTCLIFFE

"Coach Fulmer said that with the game plan we had, *somebody's band was going to be playing all day. Fortunately, we executed and it was our band playing."* —DONTE STALLWORTH ON THE 2002 CITRUS BOWL ROUT OF MICHIGAN

"Tennessee definitely has one of the best fan bases in all of football, and they travel with as many fans as anyone in the country. There are only a few schools that can compete with Vol fans, teams like Nebraska and some SEC schools travel like Tennessee, but not many. Then again I don't think you could ever hope to have any more support as a Tennessee player, from the fans that UT brings game after game. It really is amazing." —FORMER TENNESSEE OFFENSIVE TACKLE TREY TEAGUE, TO THE JACKSON SUN

"The game of football is beginning to gain a foothold in Knoxville." —KNOXVILLE JOURNAL, NOVEMBER 20, 1891

"I came here as a young kid out of high school after seeing Tennessee on TV. Even then, you could tell there was something special about Tennessee. You could tell it meant a lot to the fans, and there was a passion here. You could see and feel it on TV. I made my decision to walk on because of that passion." —DEFENSIVE COORDINATOR JOHN CHAVIS, WHO EARNED A SCHOLARSHIP AS A NOSE GUARD

"I can't tell you how proud I am of this football team and this staff, and the fight that they had. There was absolutely no panic at halftime. We talked about the heart, the toughness, representing the orange and white of Tennessee and taking charge of the football game." —COACH PHILLIP FULMER AFTER TENNESSEE'S 30–27 WIN OVER LSU IN 2005

"My advice to defensive players: take the shortest route to the ball and arrive in a bad humor." —FORMER TENNESSEE COACH BOWDEN WYATT

"I think we did have some good fortune along the way, but we also were good enough to take advantage of that good fortune. I don't know how many instances you want to talk about, but the one everyone wants to talk about is when we got the turnover against Arkansas. I think Arkansas was lucky to get a couple turnovers on us earlier in the game...the other answer to that is that with a little bit more good fortune in 1995 and 1997 this could have been our third national championship, and so we've been unlucky in that sense." —PHILLIP FULMER ON THE 1998 CHAMPIONSHIP

"Tennessee sophomores don't deserve citizenship papers until they have survived an Alabama game." —GENERAL ROBERT NEYLAND

Al Wilson

"You know, I don't know what it is about them. I just don't like Florida, period. Florida's just not my style." —DEON GRANT

"People are waiting for Tennessee to mess up, but I've got another story for them. We're not going to mess up. We have something to prove. We're on a mission." —COCAPTAIN AL WILSON, DURING THE 1998 NATIONAL CHAMPIONSHIP SEASON

"I feel somewhat validated rather than vindicated. I'm glad to get over that hurdle and win the national championship. Tom Osborne went through something similar for 18 years, and he and I talked about that. I've got a letter he sent me after the Orange Bowl, and I framed it. The last line of the letter was: 'It won't be long before you get yours,' and he was right." —PHILLIP FULMER AFTER THE VOLS WON THE 1998 NATIONAL CHAMPIONSHIP

"As great an admirer I am of Peyton Manning—and I am—I'm just as much an admirer of Tee Martin." —PHILLIP FULMER

"When we walked onto the field in 1998, I never felt we were going to lose a game. It was an attitude created by a lot of hard work and preparation." —DEFENSIVE END WILL OVERSTREET

"(Winning) the SEC championship, the SEC championship game and the national championship is actually easier to do than winning the East, and I've done them all." —PHILLIP FULMER

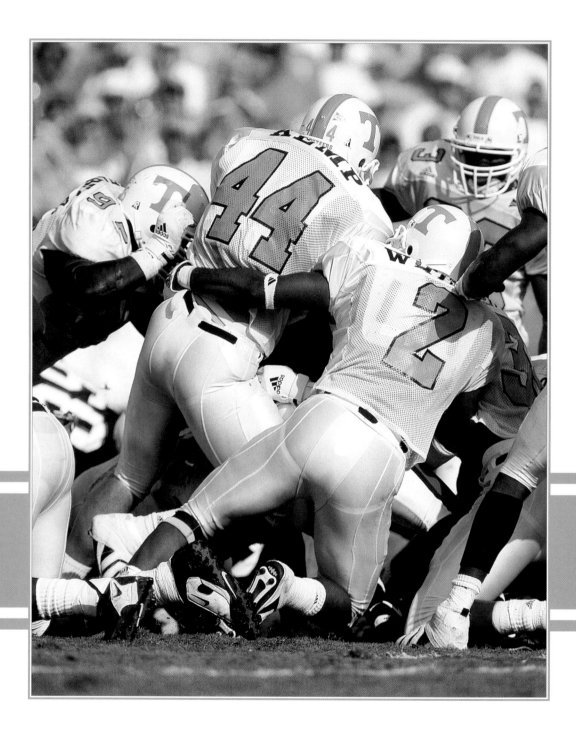

FACTS AND FIGURES

—— Tennessee ——
in the College Football Hall of Fame

NAME	POSITION	YEARS	INDUCTED
Doug Atkins	End	1950–1952	1985
George Cafego	Tailback	1937–1939	1969
Steve DeLong	Middle Guard	1962–1964	1993
Doug Dickey	Coach	1964–1969	2003
Bobby Dodd	Quarterback	1928–1930	1959 (player)
			1993 (coach)
Nathan Dougherty	Guard	1906–1909	1967
Frank Emanuel	Linebacker	1963–1965	2004
Beattie Feathers	Halfback	1931–1933	1955
Herman Hickman	Guard	1929–1931	1959

NAME	POSITION	YEARS	INDUCTED
Bob Johnson	Center	1965–1967	1989
Steve Kiner	Linebacker	1967–1969	1999
Hank Lauricella	Tailback	1949–1951	1981
Johnny Majors	Tailback	1954–1956	1987
Gene McEver	Halfback	1928–1929, 1931	1954
John Michels	Guard	1950–52	1996
Ed Molinski	Guard	1938–40	1990
Gen. Robert Neyland	Coach	1926–1934, 1936–1940, 1946–1952	1956
Bob Suffridge	Guard	1938–1940	1961
Reggie White	Defensive Tackle	1980–1983	2002
Bowden Wyatt	End	1936–1938	1972 (player) 1997 (coach)

Bob Johnson

Bowl Game Results

RECORD: 24-21

1939 Orange Bowl	Tennessee 17, Oklahoma 0
1940 Rose Bowl	Southern Cal 14, Tennessee 0
1941 Sugar Bowl	Boston College 19, Tennessee 13
1943 Sugar Bowl	Tennessee 14, Tulsa 7
1945 Rose Bowl	Southern Cal 25, Tennessee 0
1947 Orange Bowl	Rice 8, Tennessee 0
1951 Cotton Bowl	Tennessee 20, Texas 14
1952 Sugar Bowl	Maryland 28, Tennessee 13
1953 Cotton Bowl	Texas 16, Tennessee 0
1957 Sugar Bowl	Baylor 13, Tennessee 7
1957 Gator Bowl	Tennessee 3, Texas A&M 0
1965 Bluebonnet Bowl	Tennessee 27, Tulsa 6
1966 Gator Bowl	Tennessee 18, Syracuse 12
1968 Orange Bowl	Oklahoma 26, Tennessee 24
1969 Cotton Bowl	Texas 36, Tennessee 13
1969 Gator Bowl	Florida 14, Tennessee 13
1971 Sugar Bowl	Tennessee 34, Air Force 13
1971 Liberty Bowl	Tennessee 14, Arkansas 13
1972 Bluebonnet Bowl	Tennessee 24, LSU 17
1973 Gator Bowl	Texas Tech 28, Tennessee 19

1974 Liberty Bowl	Tennessee 7, Maryland 3
1979 Bluebonnet Bowl	Purdue 27, Tennessee 22
1981 Garden State Bowl	Tennessee 28, Wisconsin 21
1982 Peach Bowl	Iowa 28, Tennessee 22
1983 Florida Citrus Bowl	Tennessee 30, Maryland 23
1984 Sun Bowl	Maryland 28, Tennessee 27
1986 Sugar Bowl	Tennessee 35, Miami 7
1986 Liberty Bowl	Tennessee 21, Minnesota 14
1988 Peach Bowl	Tennessee 27, Indiana 22
1990 Cotton Bowl	Tennessee 31, Arkansas 27
1991 Sugar Bowl	Tennessee 23, Virginia 22
1992 Fiesta Bowl	Penn State 42, Tennessee 17
1993 Hall of Fame Bowl	Tennessee 38, Boston College 23
1994 Florida Citrus Bowl	Penn State 31, Tennessee 13
1994 Gator Bowl	Tennessee 45, Virginia Tech 23
1996 Florida Citrus Bowl	Tennessee 20, Ohio State 14
1997 Florida Citrus Bowl	Tennessee 48, Northwestern 28
1998 Orange Bowl	Nebraska 42, Tennessee 17
1999 Fiesta Bowl	Tennessee 23, Florida State 16
2000 Fiesta Bowl	Nebraska 31, Tennessee 21
2001 Cotton Bowl	Kansas State 35, Tennessee 21
2002 Florida Citrus Bowl	Tennessee 45, Michigan 17
2002 Peach Bowl	Maryland 30, Tennessee 3
2004 Peach Bowl	Clemson 27, Tennessee 14
2005 Cotton Bowl	Tennessee 38, Texas A&M 7

Career Statistical Leaders

Rushes—556, Travis Henry (1997–2000)

Rushing Yards—3078, Travis Henry (1997–2000)

Average per rush (min. 250 rushes)—6.67, (2089 yards, 313 rushes) Charlie Garner (1992–1993)

100-yard plus games—15, Travis Henry (1997–2000)

Rushing TDs—37, Gene McEver (1928–1931)

Rushing TDs by a quarterback—16, Tee Martin (1996–1999)

Pass attempts—1381, Peyton Manning (1994–1997)

Pass completions—863, Peyton Manning (1994–1997)

Completion percentage (min. 100 atts.)—63.0 (102 of 162) Daryl Dickey (1981–1985)

Passing yards—11,201, Peyton Manning (1994–1997)

TD passes—89, Peyton Manning (1994–1997)

Reggie White is Tennessee's career leader with 32 sacks.

Most consecutive games throwing a TD pass—18, Heath
Shuler, October 17, 1992–January 1, 1994 (1991–1993)

Lowest percentage of interceptions—(min. 150 atts.) 1.2 (2
in 162 atts.) Daryl Dickey (1981–1985)

Total rushing and passing plays—1534, Peyton Manning
(1994–1997)

Total rushing and passing yards—11,020, Peyton Manning
(1994–1997)

Highest average per play (min. 300 plays)—7.18 (11,020
yards, 1534 plays) Peyton Manning (1994–1997)

Receptions—183, Joey Kent (1993–1996)

Receiving yards—2814, Joey Kent (1993–1996)

TD catches—25, Joey Kent (1993–1996)

Most punts—204, Craig Colquitt (1975–1977)

Punting Average (min. 75 punts)—43.9, Jimmy Colquitt
(1981–1984)

Punt return average—14.7 (808 yards, 55 returns) Bert
Rechichar (1949–1951)

Kickoff return average—32.6, George Cafego (1937–1939)

Total tackles—547, Andy Spiva (1973–1976)

Sacks—32, Reggie White (1980–1983)

Interceptions—18, Tim Priest (1968–1970)

Interception return yardage—305, Mike Jones (1967–1969),
Tim Priest (1968–1970)

Most TDs by interception returns—5, Jackie Walker
(1969–1971)

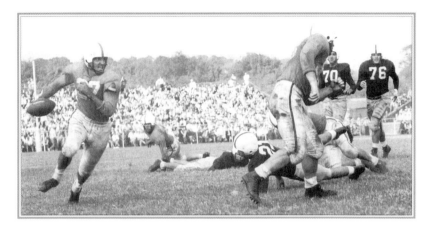

Tennessee Milestones

Undefeated and untied—1896, 1914, 1938, 1998

Undefeated, once-tied—1916, 1927, 1928, 1929, 1931, 1932

Undefeated, untied and unscored upon (regular season)—1939

Southeastern Conference champions—1938, 1939, 1940, 1946, 1951, 1956, 1967, 1969, 1985, 1989, 1990, 1997, 1998

Best season—1998, 13–0

Worst season—1906, 1–5–1, 6 points to 116

Best three-year period—1938–1940, won 30 consecutive regular season games, scored 807 points to 42

Best offensive teams—1993, 471 points in 11 games; 1990, 442 points in 11 games; 1997, 411 points in 12 games; 1998, 408 points in 12 games

Best defensive teams—1939, held 10 regular-season opponents scoreless; 1938, allowed 16 points